MY DAWAH LETTER TO PSYCHIATRISTS AND THERAPISTS

GREGORY HEARY

NO PAGE IN YOUR
BOOK OF DEEDS ON
THE DAY OF TERROR
SHOULD BE BLANK
OR WASTED WITH
SINS EVEN IF IT IS
ERASED BY ALLAH
DUE TO
REPENTANCE.

Greetings from a former ECMC Psychiatric patient from 2017 to 2023 and November 2024 to February 2026. I felt I should leave behind a parting gift for those whose valued Service I hope to have undeservedly gained benefit from. Also I attempted to arrogantly give sincere egotistical advice just in case I regret not doing so later. Sorry if these goodbye presents cause Controversy or Disrupts the ongoing Healthcare activities unnecessarily/wastefully. I also apologize if I wrote too much or wrote using unknown words above anyone's English reading level making them uncomfortable or painfully embarrassed due to not knowing certain words others might have had to define for them.

(Originally In this space I had written a few paragraphs detailing how/who would deliver my dawah gifts free of HIPAA information, they were mostly this letter combined with Hadith card decks from Ahl-Haqq Hadith Cards. Since the letter became this book then I deleted those paragraphs for this book length to be shorter.)

Now I shall list the names of who these gifts are intended to go to and I apologize if I forget anyone I met personally who still works at the ECMC clinic that I forget but Allah knows of. Don't worry I won't mention the full names of anyone just in case, for HIPAA laws are often taken more seriously in obedience as if it were more sacred than Allah's Shariah.

- **Tina** the first outpatient person I had talked to in a billable fashion after being discharged from inpatient with a psychiatric diagnosis in 2017.

- **Josh** a former therapist I had as my 2nd male therapist if I recall during 2021 who I could no longer see because he got promoted. I don't know if he still works at ECMC or not.

Regarding all my past therapists most no longer work there as far as I know, because of getting fired, retired, or quitting as it seems the therapy department at ECMC is like a revolving door; perhaps because of low pay or stress from dealing with people like me and our mental health difficulties or a mixture of both; or other various things. Also it is harder for me to check who is there and their full name spellings as well since I cannot find a ECMC therapist page. Maybe that's an intentional policy as destiny has it.

- **Dr. G** who I met at that time in 2017 in 5 zone 2 who served me three days before I rudely threatened to start a legal mental health abuse case against him due to some 4 or 5 anti-religious comments he made. One of which was that me changing religions from Catholicism to Islam 6 years earlier in 2011 was a proof I had active mental illness in 2017 and earlier because of such cultural identity instability. Since as Dr. G believed all sane people keep their parental/communal religion without ever changing it for any reason. To him all religions are false and must be kept for mental stability reasons even if one no longer believes in it since all are false/flawed and unbelievable man-made cultural byproducts anyways. Which I at the time, due to the circumstances and extra emotional instability due to a mental health crisis felt such comments were insensitively discriminatory according to even secular USA law and extremely ignorant generally and specifically as it pertained to religion overall and Islam especially. What was destined to be said was destined to be said and perhaps I misheard him or misunderstood, as he had later said. Or perhaps he was just testing me in a surprisingly unexpected perhaps legal though unorthodox way, to see how I would react to better evaluate my mental health as he later wrote when labeling me mentally ill and "simple-minded". Regardless there are no sore feelings nor explicit desire for his removal even if justified. Because if he is ignorant then what else can be expected if he isn't blessed to know any better? Or if he is unethical, as some may be tempted to investigate and as I may have suspected or rudely said aloud via backbiting in the past, crisis or not, then if he were replaced given the condition of the Psychiatric field or industry it's likely his replacement could be even more ignorant or unethical than he is. So, I don't desire to make a bad situation worse in any way if it is even actually a bad situation and I didn't misanalyse the situation, which is highly possible as a former mental health patient who has a faulty imperfect memory due to their sinful spiritual condition. I don't mean this insincerely, I think, secretly hoping actions or investigations take place despite saying the opposite using reverse psychology. But truly the potentially mistaken diagnosis with him labeling me in 3 days with a disease that requires 6 months of continuous symptoms (that I only had 3 months of maximum) was my destiny that could not be avoided in any way. And if Allah saved me from the disease of ignorance that has been destined to temporarily afflict Dr. G, or anyone/everyone on this list, then I should be obediently grateful for being saved from such a dangerous level of ignorance myself which is a much worse mental condition than those treated by all the highly trained medical experts working at ECMC. For ignorance can be even more dangerous to someone in this life and the next than hypocritical insincerity. While arrogance is worse.

Of which perhaps a reader at this point may think I have some high-level wisdom or sincerity. Whereas they only say this due to ignorance themselves of my great sinful Satanically assisted acting performances where I would publicly wear Islamic clothing like a turban, and pretend to be actively absorbed beneficially reading Islamic books in the waiting room, or pray the 5 obligatory Salat daily when necessary outside, or due to experiences as a patient. Whereas they don't know what I am arrogantly thinking inside, or sinfully doing in private where there are no other human eyes or recording devices, and I do many other sins which I will try to keep hidden like disobedience or lack of duty in fulfilling the minimum obligatory respect to my non-Muslim parents. So perhaps you only think I am spiritually above average due to being ignorant of my reality or being exposed to mostly mentally ill people who have set the spiritual standards so much lower than what our unique Creator requires as minimally expected in life.

- **Dr. E** who serviced me patiently and professionally from 2017-2023. Though she believed Dr. G's quick diagnosis after 3 days more than me, this is not her fault due to incompetence or misunderstanding of the case "facts", however accurately or inaccurately my medical chart data may be recorded. Dr G as a professional Doctor was systematically forced to give a diagnostic label for my own benefit to attempt to help me understand and qualify for the help I was desperately in need of; which I was destined to receive and eventually happily appreciate and enjoy up to now. Whether Dr. G was 100% correct or not, is not her responsibility. As for her role she had my best interests in mind I hope and cannot be blamed for the inherent Psychiatric bias unavoidable in reading a diagnosis from a trusted respectable colleague who has vast expert experience in this health field specialty. Especially given the short timeframe of appointments and that I did have legitimate mental health flaws I needed help with along with my spiritual flaws, as the two are inseparably intertwined. It is not blameworthy either if the secularist dogmatic American medical system somewhat blinds medical professionals from seeing how religion itself effects mental health and that mental health and spiritual health cannot be independent ever even if such is attempted.

The secular medical system in America is mostly attributable to our political philosopher founders' disbelief in Islam, due to lack of exposure from their own Christian culture slowly being destroyed and decaying since the Prophet Muhammad was sent. Their philosophy has destined us to have an imperfect flawed theological understanding nationally choosing secularism as an allegedly best possible alternative approach instead of any form of ignorant intolerant Christian Sectarian Government to serve as many people as possible as best as possible as quickly as possible. Simply put without the national or political governance of Prophetic Islamic Shariah guidance, due to lack of understanding/belief in Islam, what better alternative is there for us in a country with such a diversity of contradicting religious ideas? Absolute National Freedom to theoretically believe or practice any religion at all, as legally preached but not practiced in reality, is what we got stuck with. As idiotic as this freedom is religiously, it has forced the American medical system into this situation and left no easy fix to improve it better to increase efficiency for American medical staff nor American medical patient satisfaction; as Allah has destined. Not much any of us can do about it and it could be made much worse if we try unwisely rocking the boat in unprophetically approved ways too, like sinful protests, revolutions, voting, etc. Although I must address

11

one thing I have witnessed in my experience that I find disgusting and unprofessional despite the secular claims of impossibly attained religious neutrality and lack of bias or prejudice or religious discrimination.

This is the issue of "Luck" or superstitious practices like "crossing your fingers" or "knocking on wood". If you choose to play the secular game, sinful and impossible as it is, then you all can do it better. Don't say you are secular and professional and then preach superstitious religious doctrines and practices like "Luck" whether "Good" or "Bad", or make evil comments about the weather Allah controls and blesses us with, which I have witnessed being made by many in ways that are too numerous to list. This is unprofessional hypocritical sinful and medically proven to be bad practice at best being a placebo, that in reality can doom an individual patient and the medical staff to eternal hell without you even knowing it while being too ignorant to repent. If you didn't really believe such religiously significant superstitions and let your personal addictions to popular culturally common habits influence you so much that you literally cannot avoid certain phrases or actions, no matter how hard you try to do so, then at least correct yourselves publicly when you slip up and make a such a mistake. Sincerely repent using the grievous error as motivation to try avoiding it in the future when it might be harder due to others mentioning such stuff around you while you know it is so wrong and medically unprofessional and spiritually bad. Because as it is now, the ECMC system is so poisoned by such superstition that people like me get stressed over not being able to confidently correct such hypocritical unsecular medically false and spiritually wicked statements/deeds. Truly I would feel much better during my treatment and then some idiot would say something about luck or the weather and ruin my entire mind state and spiritual state due to the situation where I knew better and failed to correct it well, or attempted to correct it well and failed to do as well of a job as I am expected by Allah to do. So I got more psychological damage done to me by these unintentional innocent doctrines of "Luck" and

"Superstition" popping up than I had experienced during psychosis while in CPEP, perhaps if I am not sinfully over-exaggerating my reality.

And this is why I have decided to stop treating at ECMC primarily. It is mostly due to this issue of non-Muslims who are forced to serve in a Secular system, doing so as best they can, which is something we can't control. But they are doing so with these superstitions that I cannot correct; among other things. Personally, if HIPAA allows me to say, I am entirely physically, mentally, emotionally healthy, as I hope my former psychiatrist and therapist still agree, and even surprisingly surpassed all expectations my 2017 diagnosis implied I could possibly achieve. Many ECMC experts told me more than once after I got officially governmentally labeled as "Disabled" in 2018 that my best predicted life outcome, since I didn't want to sinfully pay USA taxes to fund the wicked immoral Kafir war machine in Afghanistan until the Muslims won, (which occurred as destined as a surprise to some in 2021, for which I was medically labeled as an "extremist" for being joyous about) was to live in a group home for mentally ill people for the rest of my life after my non-Muslim parents died. I got married in 2023, currently got multiple remote jobs and have multiple business enterprises, on my way to moving overseas to a Muslim country if Allah decrees, and have not taken any medication of the types you recognize since November 11th, 2025. I don't say this to boast and am unaware of what the scary future holds and maybe I could get worse than ever before if Allah so decrees. Yet here I just explain I'm not in a mentally ill health condition anymore, or so I think/claim as I did before when I had mental health that was poor. The other reason I stopped treatment is because I feel it is spiritually inappropriate to continue being treated by non-Muslims who are unqualified due to their personal private religions to correctly responsibly and respectfully analyze my mental health, as I hope to spiritually rise to higher potential ranks if Allah wills. Spirituality itself can be often misunderstood in the short timeframes medical staff has to work with regardless of medical professionality, good intentions, experience, communication abilities and all the rest. In fact, just 1 or 2 months before I was given confident approved permission by ECMC staff to completely safely stop brain medicine forever, (a decision I cautiously delayed to do in smaller steps for even longer to prevent "rebound psychosis" or withdrawal symptoms) I was strongly frighteningly recommended to increase my medicine dose immediately by 150% minimum due to sincere concern over my mentality because I didn't want to share my new business idea with the doctor. Surprisingly my non-Muslim mom also agreed and I would have likely been back on a very physically sedating mentally slowing dose much longer, if not for life, had Allah not protected me as decreed. This too is another flaw of behavioral health medicine in that there are no accurate methods yet to determine which medicine is best in the most accurate "minimum necessary dosage" as is often claimed to be desired. Basically, there are few brain scans or actual scientific tests that are objectively true and undebatable to ensure a perfectly executed mental health treatment for the alleged "chemical imbalance" caused by "genetics", of which the mystery causation genes do not get identified or even tested for. So, this genetic blame game and medicine dosage guesstimation is much more of a subjective religious diagnosis than any other type of medical science. Especially since the main factor affecting treatment are the words spoken by the patient and the way their medical experts understand or misunderstand those statements within a short out of context 15-30 minutes, while ignoring religion and its influence or anything unseen like Angels, Jinn, God or Sins, or communication limitations (possibly hindered by actual potential brain damage). And that is without the Secular Government making additional changes to standard practices due to political philosophies as has been done routinely. Such as the famous example where since the 1970s CE hormone therapy treatment that previously successfully cured homosexuality caused by "chemical imbalances" before politicians determined homosexuality was a "Constitutionally protected right in America, and thus the world by default as well, covered under the 'God-Given' pursuit of happiness doctrine and 'right' of consent making freedom legalize any desired sin'". This change took place despite hundreds of years of Psychiatry and Psychology labeling homosexuality and the new sexual fetishes recently spread as a mental illness caused by "chemical imbalance" and curing many patients from them. Yet now such beneficial health treatment gets called "*ignorant illegal immoral unethical malpractice discrimination*" as is known from "common sense" as democratically voted on and therefore "Divinely proven" practically as a doctrine treated more sacred than many theologies. Afterall I can criticize "mentally healthy" people eating bread and wine blasphemously saying they are eating the 100% human Prophet Jesus/God/son inspired by a "Holy Ghost" and that's just my "intolerant rude religious opinion" but if I said "Homosexuality" was a "mental illness" that is a punishable crime in this country. Whereas it's possible and even considered good medical practice for the Jesus/God wine-drinking person saying they have a ghost inside them to give me pill prescriptions to take daily that would knock out an elephant unconscious. Do you not see the theoretical insanity of the Secular ECMC medical mental health philosophies that will change with "new discoveries" made by politicians and pharmaceutical company sponsored research? All the while ignoring "religion" because that's just some cultural historically significant side-subject to be kept private and secret.

Secularist mental health medicine is flawed by design making it handicapped when attempting to benefit any allegedly spiritually developing Muslim upon the correct Islamic faith of the original Prophetic denomination or sect of Salafiyyah taught and practiced by the Sahabah. Because Islam in general forbids Muslims from accepting help from non-Muslim good doers when it is unnecessary; even in the deviant heretical diluted and popular versions of Islam often found in America and around the world. Whereas Salafiyyah being the only pure version of Islam, though it's practitioners and claimants vary vastly in their ability to practice it or explain/represent it, has even stricter standards regarding help from non-Muslim characters. In my opinion where I am now in life, the "benefits" I get from ECMC non-Muslims in a non-halal environment that is not 100% Shariah compliant no longer outweigh the harms and potential risks to me regarding my spirituality and mental health to continue to justify treatment at your fine exceptionally helpful Behavioral Health medical facilities. Maybe if Allah decrees that ratio will change and I may need help again even if I hate it and protest it in Islamic or sinful ways. Yet most of the time I just attend appointments trying to share Islamic Salafiyyah with the staff anyways, half-heartedly, as best as I pretend to myself I've tried to spread Islam; allegedly because Allah requires me to try to do so and not due to ego. Whereas I don't think it is morally justified to have Medicaid continue to pay for such a thing and if I am to pay for treatment myself, or have others like my parents pay due to not earning enough $ to require taxes that fund the Zionist Israeli Genocidal anti-Islam and anti-Christian war machine, then I'd rather Muslims advise me regarding my mental health in a Shariah compliant environment. This is much better for me spiritually and more effective regarding treatment and overall multi-layered health safety than Muslims or non-Muslims in ECMC's non-halal place that cannot be changed much due to national governmentally imposed medical laws.

So that is why I claim to be leaving ECMC forever, inshallah. Not because I was wronged any more than can be expected, or because I feel upset, nor because I am mentally unwell despite what the length of this letter may suggest. The thing I hope to have learned is that spirituality has a greater impact on health than realized, especially mental health; as I alluded to earlier with sins impacting memory recollection. Yet this is not the time for a super sermon to fully explain to people who don't have time, nor care, nor believe, nor will they remember or benefit much if they did, except if Allah decreed. I will just say how I now believe there is a special type of insanity that neither you "experts" nor myself ever believed could be a possibility for me regarding my health. At first I thought it was magic from a heretic pretending to be Muslim that I tried to get fired from a mosque, that led me to have a mental health crisis I diagnosed as "Sihr al-Junun" or "Magically induced insanity" that can occur from devils with or without magic being involved as/if Allah decrees. Yet clearly such a diagnosis is not accepted in American Secular medicine, at least not when it is self-diagnosed or at least not in my destined condition. Later I learned and accepted my health crisis could be caused by many alternative things like nutritional deficiency, stress, lack of sleep, or "genes". Though I still do not know what gene it is that is allegedly responsible for my disease, or if I have it, or if it is active, or if the gene theory is true indeed. If the seemingly unproven gene theory cause is true then I would still say it's Allah's destiny regardless of what caused my crisis whether magic or anything on this list or everything mentioned combined and something we might not yet know about or remember if we recognized. The true cause is unknown by all and we can only ever guess. Yet as I stopped some secret sins, I had hidden even from myself due to being so corrupt spiritually for so long, I got an extra medical theory. It could be possible all those causes were present but none of them are necessary to have caused the results of my health crisis. There is a potential possibility that Allah, who I know many of you don't believe in or want to hear about, could have destined my mental crisis due to knowing it would lead to a better blessing later that I could not have otherwise achieved without such harm being decreed and done to my mental/spiritual health. It doesn't need to have been magic that harmed me, even if magic was done possibly, of which when done is generally unproveable without a confession from the criminal. It could be that I was protected from magic attacks, though admittedly I didn't protect myself as best I knew I could, and nutritional imbalance, and harm from sleeplessness or stress and the alleged gene disease. Allah could have decreed I get the crisis because of Love for me that while undeserved would make me become a less evil person in the future, that I never would be if I remained healthy. All the other possible causes of my crisis could just be excuses Allah wanted to be useable and plausibly disguise the reality until I acquired this potentially true understanding,

23

eventually; undeservedly and arrogantly shared as if it were something special to me only. This crisis may have protected me from many harmful things we can prove, but all that provable benefit will be of no benefit if later I go to hellfire, eternally or temporarily if Allah destined and desires me to live/die in a state that qualifies me for such a fate. My breakthrough theory was acquired only recently after many difficult spiritual changes took place for which I will not explain much. Basically sins and hypocrisy can damage a soul so much, (which again Secular medicine doesn't officially count as existing among other things like any God(s), any Divine Revelation, any Angels, any Jinn, any Devils, any Prophets, any Paradise, any Hell; etc. limiting its effectiveness as destined), that a spiritually sick patient imagines they are sincere and doing good deeds which they can confidently prove and fool others into believing textually citing evidence very convincingly as Allah decrees some of us can succeed in doing while being blind to their own unhealthy sins and hypocrisy. Everyone is different as equality is another myth, especially regarding spirituality.

Yet I will end this topic matter by saying when you truly believe in the prophetic Salafi Islamic religion, truthfully maximizing belief and maximizing practice of it publicly and privately as if you had died and came back to life multiple times escaping from deserved eternal hellfire repeatedly due to past religious failures you didn't recognize or appropriately apprize, the surprising blessings that come from Allah to a person can boggle the mentally healthy mind. So much that if all the blessings were revealed to even truly wise, pious, healthy Salafi Muslims themselves on scholastic levels they would be concerned about the mental health of the person due to lack of experiential knowledge themselves even if they were not spiritually blinded unknowingly to see the possibilities as destined. Yet because of hoping I undeservedly got such a blessed health improvement and understanding it then comes with extra personal spiritual responsibility and duties. Doing those duties must be done just to maintain such a possible status let alone gain a higher one that may get me potential safety from what I fear in eternity and in the grave after my death before the Day of Resurrection and Terrifying Judgement, which causes me to fear your attempts to help me may harm me. Since I recognize such speech is understandably a potential warning sign of mental decline, to perhaps all who hear or read it, regardless of the facts or theories, then Allah also decreed I understand that it is impossible to help you all understand in full without Allah blessing you with such an understanding himself. Hence the purpose of this surprise gift so that I may have less of a negative grade for my soul as a result of my ECMC experiences. And maybe I am in another mental health crisis and cannot recognize it even if the new theory is possible or true. But maybe, as I egotistically hope because it makes me feel better than admitting I'm in crisis mentally or spiritually, it is one of you who Allah wants to bless more to make you grow to a higher level than I and is using me and my actions temporarily before abandoning and punishing me to help you to get your destined blessings which can be so much greater than mine, which I might or might not admit or recognize. Yet despite my wild dreams and hopes that all of you would be blessed to such an extent, I profess Allah's plans are best and such potential blessings may not be sent due to Allah wisely decreeing better events. As each individual's merits differ and impact the reality Allah alone knows about their soul inside and their destined future worldly and eternal life. Some of you may benefit much, some of you may lose much while benefitting somewhat, and it may be that I get no benefit and get cursed for talking all this talking and walking all this walk and then doing something evil later to lose all hope for eternity when my life ends. As 13:9-11 of the English translations of the Quran says,

> *All-Knower of the Unseen and the seen, the Most Great, the Most High. It is the same (to Him) whether any of you conceal his speech or declares it openly, whether he be hidden by night or goes forth freely by day. For him (each person), there are angels in succession, before and behind him. They guard him by the Command of Allâh. Verily! Allâh will not change the (good) condition of a people as long as*

they do not change their state (of goodness) themselves (by committing sins and by being ungrateful and disobedient to Allâh). But when Allâh wills a people's punishment, there can be no turning back of it, and they will find besides Him no protector.

Such a truthful statement has even been copied by the mental health industry in that things rarely ever change for the better or worse until the internal person changes and then makes external changes as a result. Often depicted as the CBT triangle but the CBT pretends the soul and heart have no role at all, making the brain be blamed for everything as the philosophers that built Greece/Rome and Euro-Merica who worship intellect over everything cited Empiricism as the only verifiable reality. Yet there are deeper realities as the mental health field cannot ignore the many cases of unexplainable possession or "magic" that they admit don't make sense or can be cured. Sadly they neither know how and why every Exorcism type can seem to work for such cases too, even if done in the name of false fake gods less real than Santa Claus. I can attest every exorcism type "seems to work" as a former Catholic Seminarian trained to be an Exorcist who surprisingly became a Salafi Muslim Fundamentalist and did limited training for Ruqya (Islamic Prophetic Exorcism) when in 2017 I had a "mental health crisis", blaming magic induced insanity from a heretic leader I was peacefully battling before coming to ECMC. This local heretical imam, was later fired from his job having himself, his wife and kids evicted from free Muslim-paid housing in 2024. Yet years earlier he falsely accused me of having a oxymoronic doctrinally impossible dual membership as an Al-Qaeda and ISIS terrorist; allegedly being both types of heretics simultaneously despite both groups fighting each other. The USA Government professionally investigated these charges more competently than expected and later declared me innocent of all such claims. Which is further proven by my past FBI background check clearance for a former job processing sensitive data for USA Passports from 2024-2025. Regardless the medical mental facts often get distorted when the patient themselves are not able to be fully trusted, and magic is not something professionally allowed to be used as a diagnostic billable insurance code for treatment even if it is the actual cause of the mental health crisis. So, the lies of non-Muslim doctrines for hundreds and thousands of years create conditions that cause vast misunderstandings during mental health emergencies that require quick decisions to be made in seconds, and labels made with sparse data and then such decisions/labels get discussed over the course of about 15 minutes every few months or so, depending on how the treatment seems to go. But what is the point of discussing these details additionally when not immediately seen as relevant or important but more emotional like an angry psychotic rant? Because whether you accept magic and devils as existing with abilities to potentially cause insanity, as will be proven later, there are other mental issues devils can cause without magic or possession involved that pertain to mental health therapy treatments.

The Prophet, said, "*When Satan (Iblis)awakens in the morning, he dispatches his troops, saying: Whoever misguides a Muslim today, I will dress him with a crown. This one will go out and say: I did not leave him alone until he divorced his wife. Satan will say: A Muslim is about to get married. This one will come and say: I did not leave him alone until he disrespected his parents. Satan will say: A Muslim is about to be good to his parents. This one will come and say: I did not leave him alone until he committed idolatry. Satan will say: You, you! Another will come and say: I did not leave him alone until he committed adultery. Satan will say: You, you! This one will come and say: I did not leave him alone until he killed someone. Satan will say: You, you! Then he will dress him with a crown.*"
 Source: Sahiḥ Ibn Ḥibbān 6189

Now answer truthfully, are the following five sinful deeds sometimes motivated by devils considered as related or sometimes overlapped with "mental health problems"?

1. Divorce.
2. Poor Family Relationships or interpersonal Communication Problems.
3. False Religious Ideas (whether peaceful/legal in Secular nations like "Luck" or not)
4. Sexual Crimes as defined by Allah, like Adultery/Fornication/Rape/Masturbation outside of lawful heterosexual marriage which doesn't have deviant sex acts in it.
5. Violent Murder of others or oneself.

Are these not things that are treated and relevant in the industry of "Mental Health"? Well these are all things invisible beings called Jinn can influence humans to do if they are bad jinn working for the jinn called Iblis or Satan. But if these "mental health" issues are not allowed to be helped by the Islamic solutions, and devils cannot be acknowledged as existing since your crude medical equipment didn't detect them then what can Secular "psychotherapy" and psychiatric medicine really do to benefit? And what are its limitations? And/or potential harms when combined in Secular settings or Islamic ignorance or worse anti-Islamic leanings that brand Islamic Salafiyyah as possible extremism?

You see now the problematic scenario someone like me was put in? I'm not saying everything is a devil's fault, because humans are typically 100% responsible for everything they do. But there is much more than just "genetics" and "chemical imbalances" at play causing mental health therapy to be needed. And for those who ignore such realities and see psychiatric pharmaceuticals and psychotherapy or other types of therapy as the full life-saving salvation medicine, they are truly not doing the best job they could in their profession. There truly is no such thing as Secular non-religious mental health improvement. Believe it or not, all behavioral health or mental health or whatever phraseology you use is not just a medical field but an actual subcategory of all religions. Every religion, even those not called religions, have something to say about "mental health" and "Behaviors". So though you may claim secularist policies you unknowingly or unadmittedly are preaching and practicing religious development. And this type of counseling is something the true God will ask you each about on the Day of Judgement. You are literally doing the important work the Prophets defined as proselytization, but you got new chemical medicines and extra scientific research to help benefit in more ways and typically take less than an hour with each patient appointment. I'm sorry if I hurt any feelings in my explanation of how you are in a religious field. Yet though you may see improvements as defined by Secular medicine, many things you have called healthy are destructively sinful by Allah's definition and are not noticed as unhealthy or even considered harmful in any way. What do I mean?

What I mean is for 8 years I've been in treatment and allegedly cured. Yet I was treating my parents very sinfully the whole time, as all witnessed and didn't even think was abnormal or bad. In fact, many might have thought I had a better family relationship than most others and might even have been a healthy example. Had I died with such a "good healthy relationship" filled with lazy disrespect I surely would have burned awhile in Hellfire not expecting it. Perhaps much wrong was hidden in my family relationship, as is common, but this lack of prioritizing perfected family treatment is because non-Muslim standards of Parental rights are practically non-existent when weighed against those Allah has given and legislated in the prophetic Shariah. There is no need to fully list my sins regarding my treatment of my relatives, as Allah knows and I hope he forgives which also becomes extremely harder to get when sins are publicized, such as in therapy or psychiatrist appointments. Plus it is not just a shame for me, but a shame for my parents to mention my sins against them. So I'd be even worse if I made public repentance in detail thus embarrassing those I already harmed. Yet I will give one example to prove how you miss so many points of improvement. Often my parents would shamefully not join me in my "private appointments". This is considered normal and understandable by ECMC and general Secular medical standards. Yet prophetically there is no such thing as privacy from one's parents, even if they are non-Muslim they are entitled to maximum respect and obedience more than a Nation's political Ruler's servant is expected to give to their leader. The only exception to the strict super honor due to kinship is that there is no obedience allowed to any creature if it involves disobeying our Creator. Which is an easy statement to say when justifying disobedience in sin, which is good, but not fully halal when done in a disrespectful sinful way due to lack of prophetic wisdom and manners being religiously disguised as Islamic. Basically, it's easy to be a sinful Muslim jerk to your parents or kin and blame it on differences of religion just causing friction. And that about defines the problem that has never been even seen as a problem during my 8+ years of treatment. Just imagine a disbeliever parent driving their son to an appointment and then the son gets to choose if they want their parent to hear what is discussed. As has happened routinely. This privacy policy literally allows people to have freedom to exclude family from helping and Allah did not give this right to anyone, so that's another Secular/Freedom problem. I will stop bashing the doctrines as much going forward since they cannot be easily changed regardless but don't you experts have "healthy mentalities" so you can put in a more perfect effort to prevent as much harmful 'sins' as possible from occurring?

For my sins against my parents could not be done all by myself, I needed accomplices to enable my sinful ways and normalize such behavior over time until I myself no longer recognized or even felt guilt while committing such crime. Just consider how many sins ECMC gets daily for every appointment where family members get excluded due to ignorant arrogance of the rights Allah gives? So, when I said how ECMC is not Shariah Compliant enough, it's in many various ways that even Muslims themselves unfamiliar with Islamic law do not know nor would they say. I understand that understaffing and patient overload may take time to learn about and help everyone as best as possible. But the point I'm leading up to is that I'm glad I learned so many things by going to ECMC. Since mental health is such a religious field that is functioning so poorly across the world, and since I struggle with Arabic to officially benefit the Islamic religion much, I decided to actually become a Mental Health Therapist myself someday inshallah. Hopefully as a marriage/family therapist working for Muslims only in a Muslim country as I clearly cannot play along with secularism. Nor am I saying this to seek a professional reference or internship/externship, or scholarship type of deal. I've cited many problems rudely in this religious medical field and am glad you helped me learn how much better mental health treatment can be done. Afterall wouldn't it be hypocritical to criticize an industry that I myself refuse to guide? This doesn't justify "joining evildoers to fix the system", which is as dumb as a "good guy" trying to become a gang leader to stop gangs from doing crime. Yet I thought you'd be interested to know how the former "mentally ill religious extremist claiming magic/devil related illness" is soon to be a professional colleague inshallah. And Ruqya is also something that can/should be incorporated with mental health treatment or therapy. Just saying, without explaining it fully logistically as this letter cannot cure every systemic illness, unless Allah facilitates such blessed improvements. You are individuals like me and not capable of controlling or changing much, except the conditions in ourselves that we hide from all even ourselves. But those inner soul sicknesses are the changes

Allah requires be made, before bigger conditions change that make the world a more blessed place. Afterall the prophetic religion was spread by Allah sending one human prophet at a time, typically all by themselves with a message that changed history for the better for the rest of time.

So with that explained semi-adequately, hopefully without much pain or time wasted, the rest of my hopefully delivered gift list is as follows.

- **Girl of Asian or Philippine appearance** who worked as intake therapist/counselor who I met with my mom **in late 2025** when I reentered the ECMC clinic desiring your helpful support to safely get off medicine in the healthiest way possible with minimal risk. I do not remember her name and apologize for ethnic descriptions.

- **My 2ⁿᵈ female intake therapist** me and my mom met **in late 2025**, who worked as a therapist but I refused to have as mine due to the Islamic Shariah forbidding non-blood relative men and women to look at, touch or be alone together. Which also leads to "poor eye contact". I think her name may be Megan or something like that and she has a Caucasian complexion, which I'm sinful to even know. Because I should have avoided seeing so much of her to even know that much if I were truly practicing Salafi Islam correctly as best as possible as I like to pretend and fool myself into claiming I'm trying to do and thinking inside.

- **Dr. B** who I met twice and enjoyed speaking with despite the red string he always seems to be wearing around his wrist indicative of an Asian superstition related to magic in false unislamic Asian religions. For which I hope he doesn't get too upset at me failing to correct privately at the time due to cowardice, then exposing the string thing here and also publicly exposing/criticizing the "*non-secular religiously significant decorative 'statutes'*" that visually seem Hinduesque to me which he has in his office. Of which none of this seemed to affect his professionality when treating me twice. I just mention it as an advice that these things contradict secularism standards ECMC alleges they preach and practice according to the letter of USA laws and excel in making extra efforts in doing so for the comfort of their patients they respectfully serve as best as they are capable of doing.

- **Tom**, my final therapist inshallah. Though if I were really sincere in his gift I would have given him something in private and in this package, even if they were the same thing. Thereby giving extra to him hiding my private charity while warning him not to tell anyone else about getting two gifts so as to reduce the potential good impression such a thing would possibly inaccurately give. Likewise even if I did do such a thing and he complied with secrecy or confessed to my generosity it still wouldn't be counted as 100% sincere because of mentioning that possibility or reality here. Truthfully there is no way to maintain sincerity or secrecy in the hopes of sincerity for Allah unless Allah grants it to someone. And don't foolishly think such a truthful doctrine is actually believed by the one which is typing it. Because nobody knows another's reality inside, even the individual themselves because we lie to ourselves unknowingly due to sins building up that blinds us to self-deception also within us from forces like wicked jinn aka devils. Although devils can be a label used for humans too, though it's not easily understood as a sane way of categorizing to most people; especially non-Muslims in a Secular mental health profession.

- **Dr. D**, my last ECMC Psychiatrist to which the same as just mentioned before with Tom's potentially sincere secret gift equally applies.

- Also, I have seen a **Hijab(Head Scarf) wearing medical professional at the behavioral health clinic with a badge, who I assume is a Sunni Muslim** at least if not Salafi herself. Despite my personal belief the Niqab is obligatory for women particularly Muslims due to clear well-known evidences I shall not criticize her. Instead, I shall recognize her honor above all the rest at ECMC as Allah acknowledges and makes obligatory for me to believe in, see and say proudly though it may make things difficult for her inside spiritually or otherwise. Even if she is a heretical non-Muslim Shiite, like the Iranian, Lebanese, Iraqi or Yemeni terrorist regimes promote who doesn't know any better herself, possibly due to ignorance currently not removed by Allah for her to understand the pure Salafi Islamic religion to her maximum capabilities Allah alone knows about. To her, assuming and hoping for the best for her although we never ever met, I say "Assalaamu aleikum wa rahmatullaha wa barakatuhu" as is her apparent right deserved for me to say. Even though we may say we believe in and obey Allah as best as we can confidently fooling ourselves according to provable textually apparent and applicable facts by Shariah standards, while Satanically assuming we are Islamic enough to be rewarded someday though claiming to others and ourselves that we don't deserve it, despite internally feeling more important than Allah the King we claim aloud and silently that we worship as Allah decrees there is no excuse for us to be so deluded in our negligence in ibada on our way to a frightening finality. I also have corrupt intentions in that I heretically hope this Hijabi Muslim can save me, instead of fully trusting in Allah, from having the medical staff who reads this letter turned book, if any, call the emergency team to pick me up after I leave and delay them from drugging me up forcefully in CPEP as happened during my first ECMC visit claiming mistakenly or correctly they are "helping my health".

As a sidenote although I had a mental crisis in CPEP in 2017, it was made worse and misunderstood as Allah decreed for me, due to religious ignorance and misunderstanding. Though the video footage is likely gone or not worth retrieving and I am untrustworthy due to history both mentally and spiritually regarding my sinfully faulty memory. If I recall correctly in CPEP when I had "crisis thoughts" I was praying an apparently valid Isha prayer at night. This normally for the physically able involves prostrating the forehead on the ground and reciting Arabic phrases including the Quran aloud. Well, I was a little louder than necessary and in crisis mode. Yet the nurses perhaps didn't understand at that time what the Isha prayer looks and sounds like when done by a self-proclaimed Muslim with a not yet admitted mental health crisis. So by uttering Arabic loudly and putting my head on the ground repeatedly in faster fashion than sincerity and concentration allows, the nurses tried to stop me physically, probably fearing for my safety. Yet Islamically it is typically forbidden to stop praying any of the 5 obligatory daily Salat until finished. Though I may have been temporarily or partially excused from the obligation of the Isha Salat due to the "crisis" not yet accepted by me. I insensitively stood my ground trying to finish my prayer going up and down. However, due to my lack of patience and awareness of the best prophetically taught reaction as would please Allah most, I acted according to the hadith of prophet Muhammad which taught that if someone other than your prophet tries to physically interrupt your obligatory prayer then push them away as gently as possible to indicate you are busy praying and will be done soon. Not once, not twice, but three times. Afterwards if they continue to try physically interrupting your obligatory Salat then you are supposed to physically fight them because they are a devil (human or jinn). Of course, at the time this hadith was spoken by the prophet Muhammad it was also in a land where Arabic was known by everyone and understood, making the context important when implementing the command. I ignorantly acted violently, more than necessary or justified, when the nurses physically were preventing me from finishing my Isha Salat probably not knowing what I was saying or doing. This was not Islamic to do and not according to the best Salafi understanding/action possible at the time, even with my mental crisis and ignorance and sinful anger combined. I knew better despite all the circumstances to act as I did, and didn't even acknowledge how fully I sinned in this way then up until the moment I typed this. Because I even took pride in my mistaken "strong faith while defending myself during Salat during a mental crisis" and boasted arrogantly of this act from then until now even sinfully reporting it in more detailed book form in a memoir I wrote about my journey to the mental crisis and potential recovery from 2012-2025. For which I also apologize for not mentioning the ECMC name as positively as is justified within. Anyways I mention this to hopefully assist medical staff in the future at ECMC and elsewhere who interact with Salafis or Muslims, in crisis or not, to hopefully aide them in our interactions with each other as we live together during our journey to the graveyard. No sore feelings from me, it was destined to occur as it has and to be upset with what Allah destined for me is unappreciative almost as much as the sins I was destined to do yet chose fully without any true compulsion though I lied to myself often saying some sins were unavoidable because of the unislamic environment in America built up throughout history that we cannot change or be upset about either.

I also apologize to the Hijabi and others as well for sinfully triggering a potentially stressful or sinful dawah scenario that will harm her or Islam or Muslims or even disbelievers or cause any evil in any way to anybody no matter how unintentional or unforeseeable it may be to me but known to Allah alone the most Just Wise Judge. Because I am sinful indeed for this dramatic selfish praise-seeking fame-wanting dawah invitation in such a fashion, no matter how sincere or well-planned or non-impactful it may be in reality when all is done. Because I already know it is impossible for all these people and/or others to embrace Salafi Islam and that my invitation even if accepted by all my targets will cause disunity and trouble in an already troubled community and workplace.

As the English interpreted translations of the Arabic Quran say in 11:116-119,

> *"If only there had been among the generations before you persons having wisdom, prohibiting (others) from Al-Fasâd (disbelief, polytheism, and all kinds of crimes and sins) in the earth, (but there were none) - except a few of those whom We saved from among them! Those who did wrong pursued the enjoyment of good things of (this worldly) life, and were Mujrimûn (criminals, disbelievers in Allâh, polytheists, sinners). And your Lord would not have destroyed the cities unjustly while their people were reformers. And if your Lord had so willed, He could surely have made mankind one Ummah [nation or community (following one religion i.e. Islâm)] but they will not cease to*

So, I know in advance some people are doomed to eternal hell and me sending this message will give them less of an excuse that day, yet I selfishly hope to be one of those "reformers" while hiding hypocrisy deep inside that I lied to myself isn't there, as the Munafiqeen do when preaching Islam for the sake of Satan claiming its done for Allah alone and to cause unity upon the truth that is better than fictional unity upon falsehood. Of which disunity with some upon truth and others upon falsehood is still better than the fictional fantasy of unislamic community unity. That is what I claim I want but Allah will judge my true reality later publicly on Judgement Day.

Likewise I don't want to quote the best Quran verses to prove it's truth, because I am lazy to do so in reality. Though I can persuasively hide by saying I'm cowardly, or unwise, or don't want to waste your time reading more than necessary, or overload you with too much spiritual medicine all at once thus causing a dangerous faith overdose that causes you to get upset or spiritually sick reacting sinfully simply due to my poor selection of Salafi medicine dosage miscalculations. Even though I had a couple extra points to make I see further effort may hurt the goal of pleasing Allah the most in the best way as I can. Whereas my time has more potential value to Allah by fully exerting myself in other efforts despite my personal preference to do a fully perfect job. Maybe my perfect job is worse than that which Allah planned and/or mercifully Allah saves me from wasting more time than necessary. Or maybe I have lost the blessing of Allah due to an unknown sin or flaw so Allah took away my role and is planning to replace me with a more pure and obedient truly Salafi worshipper.

As a tip I will include a Quranic verse about insanity caused by jinn that definitely proves there are types of insanity not currently officially accepted by ECMC or Secular medicine at this current time due to disbelief and Allah's destiny.

As the English interpreted translations of the Arabic Quran say in 2:275,

> ***"Those who do dealings with usury/interest cannot stand [on the Day of Resurrection] except <u>as one stands who is being beaten by Satan into insanity</u>. That is because they say, "Trade is [just] like usury/interest." But Allāh has permitted trade and has forbidden usury/interest. So whosoever receives an admonition from his Lord and stops eating Ribâ (usury) shall not be punished for the past; his case is for Allâh (to judge); but whoever returns [to Ribâ (usury)], such are the dwellers of the Fire - they will abide therein."***

Additionally, although these are "quotes" of Quran in some sense they are not in Arabic and thus not 100% divine revelation of Allah, except for those heard in the audiobook. English translations are not sacred verses themselves or "Holy" though the meanings here are potentially sent from above the throne above the Heavens. So don't worry if the pages are damaged or anything like that because the Quran is an Arabic book. Even if some Muslims are confused or don't know better. Only Allah can accurately translate Allah 100% accurately, just as a fish cannot translate a human work, or I cannot even translate myself into another language because even while seeing what I myself wrote in any book, I will not remember what I 100% intended when I wrote English words myself at that time due to my memory flaws sinfully caused and natural human deficiencies which are known by all; but not mentioned due to my pride and insincerity not wanting to make my sins' impact on my memory fully realized by you all though I mention it repeatedly. The term "Holy Quran" is an illegal term of heretical innovation in imitation of fake scriptures promoted by non-Muslims (disbelievers) for "Holy" is an English word not even equivalent to descriptions that Allah described the Quran with himself like: ""Glorious" (Majid/Karim), "Clear/Manifest"

(Mubeen), "Honorable/Noble" (Karim), "Wise" (Hakim), "Truth" (Haqq), "Light" (Nur), "Guidance" (Huda), "Mercy" (Rahmah), and others. So, relax about the quoted verses on these pages if anything "disrespectful" is destined to occur to them. The Quran is not "Holy" even if in Arabic, as important and special as it is. Such labels like "Holy Quran" or even more accurate ones are a technically inaccurate mix/mash of multiple languages combined that violate the rules of speech and communication. The Quran is an Arabic word known to us only in the Quran due to the Quran naming itself the Quran, a fact many who believe in it don't even understand fully as Allah has destined. And now Allah has given me an extra blessed idea inshallah so as to maximize benefit in ways my best plan did not imagine. As stated before (edited out for the book version) I would give this package to my favorite receptionist, with this multi-page letter inside of about 40 regular sized pages. Yet I know it would be difficult even if possible for all the gifts to be distributed, for the letter to benefit all to whom it was addressed or anyone else who Allah had destined to receive blessings due to exposure from Naseehah upon Salafiyyah. Because one letter, is still physically limited by space and time hindering the ability for it to do goodness, as only one person can hold and read it at a time. Plus it is impractical to have the receptionist make copies of the letter or print so many pages from my home printer. So what is the solution?

As an author, I can just write this letter in book form making some edits/tweaks and have them delivered to my intended recipients saying or labeled as: "***This is a gift free from HIPAA data from a former patient wanting to show appreciation for your service to them. They just beg for your forgiveness and hope you accept this gift, and read it on your personal time safely at home or during lunch or sometime when you are not on time that ECMC pays you for.***" With my name carefully cut out of the paperback cover, title page and not even placed on the spine, so it is a gift that can be taken home by American medical staff as no HIPAA data is on or in the book as far as I know. And even if it was, written permission/consent invalidates any HIPAA law applicability anyways. And this book is definitely consensually written.

Additionally, I ask you for forgiveness for my sinfulness and insincerity in our interactions together whether you know of it or not, care or not, because Allah knows much more and has hidden the full reality of our condition for a little while more. And we can never know the full reality of our life anyways because Allah alone is qualified to know what Allah knows. Literally you have to be Allah to even know what Allah has told you and understand it accurately correctly even if Allah told you everything in full detail making it possible for you to remember it all. So due to that fact then there is definitely a big margin of error I need to request you forgive me for, though you may not fully be aware of the noble powerful rights you give up if you ever forgive me before the Day the Divine Court Session is held on the Day of Terror when all of us are stingy with our deeds that will be our only currency for any claims from those we wronged in our lives.

The other notable mentions who I intend to receive this letter/book are:

- **Joe**, at outpatient reception, the only receptionist whose name I remember because it has so few letters, making it easier on me because my sins make my memory lack recollection ability. Also because Joe usually always goes above and beyond in his job and, no offense intended, seems the most genuine and intellectual out of all the 22 Psychiatrists and 10 or so Therapists I have encountered, with only 1 Muslim psychiatrist being the exception that I met outside of the ECMC network being higher on my graded healthcare professional list than Joe the receptionist.

- The **blonde Caucasian Football fanatic Receptionist female** who can never seem to remember my name, as far as I can tell, despite not many patients wearing a Turban every time they come. Though this is indicative of sins negatively impacting her memory, it is not a flaw of hers in my view because it humbles me greatly helping me feel less arrogant than I already do every minute of every day showing me just how little I am worth to Allah's creatures and how little value I really have in Allah's opinion when he knows much worse about me than they do. If despite my great religious acting skills you cannot remember me or my name then what about Allah out of all the trillions of creatures he created when I am raised and expectedly hope for one of the best spots in eternal paradise? Realistically I don't even think I will manage to sign in on the Paradise last booked/occupied residence, or so I claim on this letter at least.

- **The darker skinned male receptionist with creative hairstyles working at the MAP clinic registration.** Another super employee like all of you at ECMC whose name I don't remember due to my sins harming memory.

- **The white skinned guy receptionist that sometimes sits on the far end of the four-corner receptionist cage** whose name I

don't remember who sometimes validates
the free parking ticket when I rudely request it
after a rudely worded appointment process
and unappreciative experience amounting to
ingratitude of a sinful level.

My last bit of advice to the reader of this letter is
to sincerely read the Quran in a language where
the message is accessible to you. I promise you
will not be disappointed and will benefit
immensely as Allah decrees. It can be read
cover to cover in just a few hours within 1 day.
Memorized in full in Arabic by millions, believed
in by billions today and uncountable numbers
throughout history as the final and only available
book from our exclusively unique one and only
Creator, named in Arabic as Allah. This book was
introduced to earth 1,420+ years ago when a 40-
year-old man in the desert of Arabia, who did not
know how to read any language or write any
language, began to claim an Angel called Gabriel
told him to repeat after him(Gabriel) what he was
being told to say which was an alleged
message/verses of a book from the Creator of
the Universe. These verses would occasionally

be revealed in various ways on various occasions for 23 more years as Muhammad's prophethood developed from lone preacher to head of state ruling over the entire Arabian Peninsula by his death in 632 CE. When this great leader died, he ruled over what today comprises the 7 different countries of Saudi Arabia, Yemen, Oman, UAE, Qatar, Bahrain and Kuwait. The enemies of prophet Muhammad were many, and still are, yet at the time they included the Roman Empire and Persian Empire superpowers as well as fake Muslim hypocrites who converted publicly while plotting against him hoping to return Arabia to paganism. Of which Muhammad soundly eliminated paganism in Arabia peacefully and militarily. Muhammad transformed Arabian society from uncivilized to role models for civilization all while functioning at a "ultra-advanced mental capacity" as head of a state he built as an asylum seeker in a foreign city of 99% non-Muslim population. Muhammad ruled for 10 consecutive years dying peacefully at 63 lunar years old while head of state, two years after eating from a poisoned sheep meant to test his prophethood according to the Jewish poisoner who embraced Islam after the event, as did many of his would-be assassins; and many of his former character assassins like myself.

I will not give a full biographical history but I will share a couple details because as "Professionally trained mental health experts" I'm confident you will find the "case history" fascinating when determining, the "mental health diagnosis" of the most influential person in history, Muhammad. But let me share a few relevant details of the case history to help you all better determine if he had a mental illness when claiming prophethood at the age of 40. Prior to his "Angelic Revelation experience" Muhammad was known by his family and the entire city by the nickname of "The Trustworthy" (Al-Amin) due to his exemplary well-known famous wise justice and truthful honesty.

Muhammad's father died before he was born around the year 570 CE. Muhammad's mother died when he was 6, making him a double-orphan without parents at all. So, his grandfather took him in to raise Muhammad, then Muhammad's grandfather died when he was 8. He was then raised by his Uncle Abu Talib until Muhammad grew up and got married at the age of 25. His first wife at that time was 40, she was about 15 years older and gave birth to all his kids that survived childhood (4 girls, and 3 boys total; with some of those boys being from other women later). Yet none of his boys survived childhood. And only 1 daughter of Muhammad outlived him, Fatima, who died 6 months after he did as he prophesied on his deathbed that she would unexpectedly and unknowably be the first relative of his to die after him. Prior to the auditory revelation occurring unexpectedly without warning, Muhammad said that the first "symptom of prophethood" that started happening was every night he slept and dreamed, then on the next day the same exact things he dreamed of would occur exactly as he vividly dreamed before they actually took place.

Later Prophet Muhammad explained this is due to the pre-written destiny of Allah called Qadr, sometimes shown to people, believers and disbelievers alike, as their soul is taken out during sleep beginning to ascend to Allah above his throne. Muhammad taught there are 3 categories of dreams.

1. True Dreams from Allah which are still possible today and 1/46th of prophecy or about 2% and all that is left of it today that is possible for people to attain, often misunderstood or mislabeled as "Déjà vu".

Dreams are another topic mental health experts fail to explain, since they are not well studied by modern medical machines.

As it is reported in some hadith with this one by Abdullah bin Umar: *"When one sleeps deeply, his soul ascends. If it reaches the Throne before waking, that dream is true. If it wakes before reaching, then it is not."* Source: Mustadrak al-Hakim Hadith (8199)

These are experiences, I'm confident many of you have experienced, thereby proving to you in your own life that supernatural realities secular mental health disbelieves, like pre-known destiny, are real. But then some blasphemously talk about stuff like "Luck" and superstitious practices that all contradict the reality of pre-written divine destiny of Qadr proven by experiences you testify to the reality of like "Déjà vu".

2. Dreams from Devils trying to harm, frighten, or suggest evil thoughts to harass you while asleep.

The Prophet Muhammad said:
"If anyone sees a good dream, it is from Allah. He should thank Allah and share it. But if the dream is disturbing, it is from Shaytan; seek refuge in Allah and do not share it—it will not harm him."
Source: Mustadrak al-Hakim Hadith 8181

3. Dreams that are about what you were already thinking about while awake, these don't mean much at all but are just like recycled thoughts being digested.

Muhammad would tell these "True Dreams" to his wife and daughters when he woke up and then later during the same day they would occur exactly as he described earlier without possibly controlling or manipulating events to pan out with an exactly matching or even closely matching result. Then for 2 years, more intensely during the 6 months before meeting Angel Gabriel, Muhammad would auditorily hear trees or stones distinctly say his name with respectful greetings when nobody else was around to hear it. When hearing these greetings in isolated circumstances Muhammad was unable to be able to talk back to them and these inanimate objects would not say anything further than a respectful greeting by name. Muhammad never worshipped idols, nor drank wine or tried any intoxicants, nor even listened to the scientifically highly graded intoxicant of music at a wedding or other functions. He once attended a wedding trying to enjoy music but passed out unexplainably several times and decided to stay away from listening to music ever afterwards. Of which as a former Christian Rapper with 4 commercial Hip-Hop albums and a Niagara County Community College degree in professional music production, where we got taught how/why music is an intoxicating drug that changes brain chemistry, I fully understand why Allah would protect someone from such a powerful harmful drug like music. Though currently ECMC and the health industry refuses to accept music is a drug due to their religious and scientific disbelief. This refusal for Secular medicine to classify music as the intoxicating drug it is compares with how cigarettes or tobacco used to be cool and healthy/medicinal. And that drug fact is about non-lyrical music without wicked lyrics preached by sinful people promoting crime that wouldn't be allowed to be preached otherwise without "fun exciting relaxing musicality", even with freedom of speech legalizing nearly all wicked speech. Sadly in the mental health field if anyone even suggests things like pornography or music can damage mental health whether they are addictions or not, many psychiatric experts would say such a statement is psychotic itself and have plenty of brain changing medicines to fix such "abnormal crazy thoughts". Because of "professionally educated secular non-religious non-biased genuine concern". Do you think I would quit a lucrative Christian Rap career and destroy hundreds of my personal rap music cd collection, avoiding music like the plague despite how difficult that is to do given music's global popularity if I didn't have 100% undeniable proof music is a sinful drug? Am I dumb? Or are you, just addicted to music so much already you don't want to hear the truth? Yet as "religiously accommodating" as ECMC is how often is a music-free environment created so Muslims at ECMC can feel they are not sinful being brainwashed by force because of democratic popular vote or unislamic culture saying music is harmless and helpful? Why do you force us to listen to sinful music during inpatient therapy sessions or waiting areas? Is it a marketing tool to brainwash consumers increasing purchases like the stores use it for? Is it that the more music is heard in the hospital the higher the healthcare bill? If so, then isn't that a proof that music is dangerous, unhealthy and sinful? If music is played on hospital property just for popular cultural addiction reasons, then how "religiously accommodating" are you actually being? Especially when every song has a different sinful religiously themed message designed to convert its listeners to certain types of emotions, thoughts and behaviors making every song a type of CBT therapy from sinners.

After claiming an invisible being (yet to be known as Angel Gabriel) had told Muhammad to repeat certain words when he was contemplating the pitiful state of the popular idiotic idol worship of Mecca and Arabia alone in a cave, Muhammad returned to his wife of 15 years afraid he was insane or attacked by a Jinn/Devil. Muhammad told his wife something came to him and asked him to read. He said he replied, "I do not know how to read." Muhammad continued (the following wording from a later report after it was known to have been Angel Gabriel):

"Then the Angel held me (forcibly) and pressed me so hard that I felt distressed. Then he released me and again asked me to read, and I replied, 'I do not know how to read.' Thereupon

he held me again and pressed me for the second time till I felt distressed. He then released me and asked me to read, but again I replied. 'I do not know how to read.' Thereupon he held me for the third time and pressed me till I got distressed, and then he released me and said,

> **'Read, in the Name of your Lord Who has created (all that exists)! He has created man from a clot (a piece of thick coagulated blood), Read! And your Lord is the Most Generous. Who has taught by the pen, has taught man that which he knew not."**
> (Quran translated 96:1-5).

Muhammad returned frightened from that experience; and the muscles between his neck and shoulders were trembling till he came upon Khadija (his wife, 55 years old at the time) and said, "*Cover me!*" She covered him, and when the fear was gone, he said to Khadija, "*O Khadija! What is wrong with me? I was afraid that something bad might happen to me.*" Then he told his wife the story. Khadija said, "*Nay! But*

receive the good tidings! By Allah, Allah will never disgrace you. *For by Allah, you keep good relations with your Kith and kin, speak the truth, help the poor and the destitute, entertain your guests generously and assist those who are stricken with calamities."* Khadija took Muhammad to Waraqa bin Naufil, the son of Khadija's paternal uncle. Waraqa had converted to Christianity, became a Christian Scholar and was one of the few non-pagans in the city of Mecca. Waraqa was an old blind man who had lost his eyesight. Khadija said (to Waraqa), *"O my cousin! Listen to what your nephew is going to say."* Waraqa said, *"O my nephew! What have you seen?"* The Prophet Muhammad described whatever he had seen. With deep seriousness Waraqa bin Naufil said, *"This is the same Angel (Gabriel) who was sent to Moses. I wish I were young and could live up to the time when your people would turn you out."*
Muhammad said, *"Will they turn me out?"*

Waraqa replied in the affirmative and said:
"Never did a man come with something similar to what you have brought but was

But after a few days Waraqa died. After 13 years, following his prophethood being publicly known and believed in and/or disbelieved in, the first Islamic Nation was established in Medinah. At the time in his hometown of Mecca, Muhammad had a 100 camel bounty put on his head where they started killing Muslims after years of abuse and total economic/social/cultural boycott and illegal government sponsored torture didn't stop Islam from spreading. So, Muhammad had to flee as a refugee seeking asylum in Medinah. In Medinah Muhammad was selected to be leader in 622 CE, without vote or objection due to pure moral character, when Muslims were less than 1% of the population numbering about 112 Muslim men in a city of 4,000 pagan polytheist men and about 2,000 Jews who were living in Medina, Arabia believing in a prophecy from prior prophets and scriptures that said a prophet would be sent to live in that city.

This Scriptural prophecy was so popular and authentic the Jews in Medinah for decades would threaten their Arab pagan neighbors in arguments warning them that they would be unstoppable once "the awaited prophet promised by God's Jewish prophets comes to this city". Many Jews in Medinah, especially Rabbinical Scholars, eventually accepted Muhammad as "that prophesized prophet". But then other Jews were racist saying because Muhammad is a descendant of Abraham via Ishmael then it cannot be him, so some other prophet of Jewish Israeli blood is supposed to be sent to Medinah instead as the prophetic Scriptures allegedly say or mean. Later the bibles were heavily edited and mistranslated to remove some things as Jews and Christians keep editing the many different bibles on the market today all of them claiming to do so due to "direct guidance from the Holy Ghost".(without getting any psychiatric medicine prescribed to them or lifelong diagnoses while drinking wine in churches playing music worshipping a human Prophet/Ghost/Father in a unexplainable mystery deity using the pagan phrase "trinity" to label it) Even Saul/Paul knew of this Medinah Scriptural prophecy. In the Biblical New Testament of Galatians after the false prophet Saul's "New Revelation about Jesus" in Damascus, Syria Saul/Paul wrote that he went directly to Arabia for years before ever going to Jerusalem to meet the "super-apostles"(actual companions of Jesus who Paul never saw in person) who Paul later contradicted and denounced as heretical hypocrites in the New Testament. Of which 52% of the New Testament is Paul's alleged writings (not all actually Paul but some are forgeries in Paul's name) which are the oldest Christian texts written though not arranged in chronological order ever and some "gospels" exist despite Paul's letters saying not to follow any gospel other than the one he preached before those 4 popular Gospels were ever written and put out of chronological arrangement in the New Testament compilation that Emperor Constantine ordered in the 300s CE, finalized in the 400s CE; debated until today. In the Bibles available today, Paul still says he spent years in Arabia before preaching Christianity once, after his "Jesus Vision", but we are focusing on Muhammad's mental diagnosis in this not Saul/Paul's. Yet Saul/Paul never says what he was doing in Arabia for several years, or who he was looking for and most Christians don't even know or get told the biblical book of Galatians written by Paul has this confession of prophet-hunting in Arabia for years. Which biblically happened between Saul's terrorist days of killing the original followers of Jesus before going to preach to gentiles in a Greek language none of the companions of Nabatean Aramaic speaking Jesus, or Hebrew Jews, or followers of Jesus could understand; with his new name of Paul making it less easy for the Muslim followers of Jesus to stop Saul/Paul from preaching heresy in Jesus' name in foreign countries in a Greek language they did not know. Especially considering they were mostly poor illiterate uneducated people themselves in a highly hostile land ruled by a Pagan Roman Empire, surrounded by an intolerant Jewish minority. Thus, keeping track of Saul/Paul speaking/writing in Greek in faraway foreign lands after a multi-year prophet-hunting vacation wasn't exactly the top priority for the

Muslim followers of the 100% human Muslim Prophet Jesus who taught Islamic monotheism just as all the Muslim prophets before him did; like prophet Abraham who was neither Jew nor Christian. Yet that's just my Muslim understanding, I'm sure Christians of which 75% don't ever read the contradictory bible once in their life, know more than me when they go to church once in a while listening to "fun songs" and watching "epic movies/TV" that I don't believe in because I'm "too religious obsessively learning via books/lectures". What do I know about religion to ever be "more correct" than those "religion experts" or their "Super Holy Christian Preachers" who put on an entertaining concert once a week quoting maybe 5 verses from different places from their special bible that so few read and all other Christian denominations say wasn't written accurately because "the Holy Ghost" is only with one Christian group and not that one? Afterall I, the Salafi Muslim guy who converted from Christianity, was diagnosed with an incurable lifelong "mental illness" that requires daily brain medicine for the rest of my life or I will be "mentally sick and unhealthy". Or at least that's what I heard from nearly all of you for 8 years 5+ months at ECMC as you got paid top dollar to tell me due to "genuine concern for my health and improvement" maybe even more than the other less special, peaceful and polite patients get.

Anyways as Head of State(the most effective in all of history according to non-Muslim history scholars), Prophet Muhammad was asked how the experience of "Divine Revelation" occurred when he would learn new verses of the Quran by Harith bin Hisham:

"How does the Wahi (inspiration) come to you?" Harith bin Hisham asked.

Muhammad said: *"At times it comes to me like the ringing of a bell and that is most severe for me and when it is over I retain that (what I had received in the form of Wahi), and at times an Angel in the form of a human being comes to me (and speaks) and I retain whatever he speaks."*

And regarding the occasional times that an "Angel in the form of a human being" came to

Muhammad, several times these incidents were seen by onlookers that numbered in the dozens or hundreds and sometimes less than dozens. During those times this "human form" would be assumed by onlookers to be a normal human from out of town that nobody else recognized or knew personally, although despite being a stranger to everybody, indicating they must be from a very far away land, this "angel in human form" would be in clean spotless clothes with no signs of fatigue or any disgusting human features like wounds or sweat or bad smells.

Umar ibn al-Khattab reported:

> *"We were sitting with the Messenger of Allah, peace and blessings be upon him, one day, a man appeared with very white clothes and very black hair. There were no signs of travel on him and we did not recognize him. He sat in front of the Prophet, rested his knees by his knees, and placed his hands on his thighs. The man said, "O Muhammad, tell me about Islam." The Prophet said, **"Islam is to testify there is no God but Allah and***

Muhammad is the Messenger of Allah, to establish prayer, to give charity, to fast the month of Ramadan, and to perform pilgrimage to the House(in Mecca) if a way is possible. *" The man said, "You have spoken truthfully." We were surprised that he asked him and said he was truthful. He said, "Tell me about faith." The Prophet said,* **"Faith is to believe in Allah, His angels, His Books, His Messengers, the Last Day, and to believe in destiny, its good and its harm.** *" The man said, "You have spoken truthfully. Tell me about Sincerity." The Prophet said,* **"Sincerity is to worship Allah as if you see Him, for if you do not see Him, He surely sees you.** *" The man said, "Tell me about the final hour." The Prophet said,* **"The one asked does not know more than the one asking.** *" The man said, "Tell me about its signs." The Prophet said,* **"The slave-girl will give birth to her mistress and you will see barefoot, naked, and dependent shepherds compete in the construction**

of tall buildings.” Then, the man returned and I remained. The Prophet said to me, **“O Umar, do you know who he was?”** *I said, “Allah and His Messenger know best.” The Prophet said,* **“Verily, he was Gabriel who came to teach you your religion.”**

Source: Sahiḥ Muslim 8

Ibn Umar reported:

A man asked the Prophet: “Which places are worst?” The Prophet said, **“I will not know until I ask Gabriel (the angel).”** *Then he asked Gabriel, and he said, “I will not know until I ask Michael.”*

(The angel) Michael came, and he said, “The best places are the mosques, and the worst places are the markets.”

Source: Sahih Ibn Hibban 1599 Grade: Hasan

So what is your diagnosis of those hundreds of other Muslims who said they visibly sometimes saw the “Angel in Human form” but didn’t know it was an angel until Prophet Muhammad told them after he left and then nobody could ever find that person no matter where they looked for them. Did they all have mental illnesses too? Some kind of a contagious mental illness multi-person hallucination? That coincidentally is a one-time event that has no other effect at all in life except for new religious beliefs of great morality and theological principles unexplainably pure and complex for the 600s CE? Do normal mental illnesses function in a question/answer format and sometimes not have answers to the questioner so the illness askes another illness to answer for them? Then the illness reports back to the patient what the 2nd illness told them to answer the question? What about the miraculous events on the field of military battles, like the Battle of Badr, between Islam and Arab Pagan Polytheism where both the Muslims and non-Muslims reported they saw "human form angels" in very extremely detailed descriptions with the colors of their turbans, horses and weapons described fighting non-Muslims despite the Muslim army only having 2 human horse units total in the battle of Badr? These "Soldier Angels in Human form" were not seen or heard by most human Muslim soldiers in those armies, nobody knew the identity of them or saw them at all before or after despite the corpses of the pagan enemies they killed being left behind. Most reports of the "Soldier Angels" were made by the non-Muslims themselves. Was that all fantasy? Or historical lies agreed upon by both Muslim and non-Muslim historians of Arabian military history at that highly religious time and environment where the losing pagans decided to say angels, not demons, where fighting against them causing them to lose to Muslims who they outnumbered and out equipped? Or do you just not have enough information to diagnose Muhammad? What about the other human Muslim non-prophet contemporaries of Muhammad who 100% eventually believed Muhammad was a Prophet despite many personally hating and fighting him in military battles for decades? What is their mental illness for eventually believing this "potential patient" was literally getting information from the Creator of Earth visibly in their presence? These Muslim eye-witnesses who saw Muhammad "getting inspired with divine revelation" described the process in their own words as follows:

Aishah (Muhammad's wife after Khadijah died) said: *Verily I saw the Prophet being inspired divinely on a very cold day and noticed the sweat dropping from his forehead (as the Inspiration was over).* Source: Sahih al-Bukhari 2

And Aishah was also the only wife who the Prophet said he would get Divine Revelation from Allah with while under the covers in the same bed as her. The Prophet thought this was because of her supreme religious character and perhaps because she was his only virgin wife when they married, as all the rest he ever married were widows or divorcees and he never got Divine Revelation when in their beds. So, is this a special mental illness that only occurs symptomatically in certain beds with certain wives but not with others?

Also, sometimes Angel Gabriel would have an appointment time with Prophet Muhammad and not show up at the scheduled agreed upon time.

Maimunah, another wife of the Prophet Muhammad, reported him as saying:

> *Angel Gabriel promised to visit me last night, but he did not visit me. Then it occurred to him that there was a puppy dog under his bed. So, he ordered and it was turned out. He(Muhammad) then got water in his hand and sprinkled it on its place. When Gabriel met him, he said: We do not enter a house which contains a dog or a picture(of animate creatures).*

So is this a special mental illness that tells you in advance when it will show up so everyone can prepare to see you get psychotically symptomatic at a specific minute of the day? And then it doesn't happen on time. Then you tell the dog to get out of the house and clean the mess up. Then the illness comes and says that they cannot come to afflict you if there is a dog in the house or a picture of any animate creature? And then this "delusional theory" gained from the "psychosis thoughts gotten from the illness" actually works and is testable to be true 100% of the time just as "the illness" said about itself?

Zaid bin Thabit reported: That the Prophet dictated to him(Quran verse 4:95): *"Not equal are those of the believers who sit (at home) and those who strive and fight in the Cause of Allah."*

 Zaid added: Ibn Um Maktum (the blind elderly Muslim man appointed as the public Athan caller announcing the daily prayer times) came while the Prophet was dictating to me and said, "O Allah's Messenger! By Allah, if I had the power to fight (in Allah's Cause), I would," and he was a blind man. So, **Allah revealed Quran to his Prophet while his thigh was on my thigh, and his thigh became so heavy that I was afraid it might fracture my thigh. Then that state of the Prophet passed and Allah revealed:-- "Except those who are disabled (by injury or are blind or lame etc.)."** Source: Sahih al-Bukhari 4592

Does this sound like any unhealthy mental symptoms you know or have heard of in your vast collective mental illness experiences? This multi-party temporary experience of extremely pious trustworthy moral humans of "Divine Revelation" that results in 3 Quran verses allegedly from Allah our Creator that says in unmatchable Arabic poetic prose:

As the English interpreted translations of the Arabic Quran say in 4:94-96,

*"O you who have believed, when you go forth [to fight lawfully with strict morality and caution to avoid sin, civilian or non-combatant injuries, or unnecessary property damage as part of a Muslim government military unit during warfare] in the cause of Allāh, investigate; and do not say to one who gives you [a greeting of] peace,
"You are not a believer," aspiring for the goods of worldly life; for with Allāh are many acquisitions. You [yourselves] were like that before; then Allāh conferred His favor [i.e., guidance] upon you, so investigate. Indeed, Allāh is ever, of what you do, Aware. Not equal are those of the believers who sit (at home), except those who are disabled (by injury or are blind or lame), and those who strive hard and fight in the Cause of Allâh with their wealth and their lives. Allâh has preferred in grades those who strive hard and fight with their wealth and their lives above those who sit (at home). Unto each, Allâh has promised good*

(Paradise), but Allâh has preferred those who strive hard and fight above those who sit (at home) by a huge reward. Degrees of (higher) grades from Him, and Forgiveness and Mercy. And Allâh is Ever Oft-Forgiving, Most Merciful.

Are those words of rhythmic Arabic psychotic nonsense happening to an active popular Head of State surrounded by hostile nations on all sides who is nearby his advisors who are also so afflicted with psychosis that they memorize these "Divine verses" and spread them all throughout the world as Shariah law where these same exact verses are memorized until this day by Arabs and non-Arabs, some of whom don't even know the meaning of what they memorized but were still able to memorize it in Arabic with perfect punctuation? If spoken by a non-Arab, while leading prayer not looking at any reference to make sure they are saying the correct words or pronouncing it correctly, the native Arabic speaking listeners would be completely oblivious as to the reciter in prayer not knowing the meaning of the verse they are perfectly pronouncing. Is this how psychotic delusional mental illnesses operate? Via contagion that spreads faster than Covid with the only side effects being that all those afflicted become better in morality and more religious and less tolerant of other religions that are false in the eyes of everyone except their own adherents, so they get a bit more preachy but not in an illegal, violent, or rude way like all the other crazy religious fanatics? What's the diagnosis from the mental health expert professionals? Is there a unanimous conclusively 100% certain consensus that cannot be overruled or revisited? Is this a mental illness Muhammad had which was in his genes triggered by Stress, Drugs, Nutrition, Age, etc.? Or was Muhammad afflicted with a demon like the Christians say so loud and commit genocide to fight against due to their "superior morals" based on "the special Holy Bible(inspired by that Holy Ghost who had over two dozen different authors write for it and hundreds of others translate for it and continues to edit this "One and Only Holy Bible", you know the one I mean right? The "most popular book in the world of all time" (just like Santa Claus goes to every kids house in the world everywhere in 1 night every year) But it's not exactly the same edition as the new one which President Donald Trump, who prays God blesses America and everywhere else so loudly, just published a new version of with the anti-religious contradictory still being amended and edited America political scriptures included.) that Christians hundreds of years later apologize for profusely, as with the Crusades past, present and ongoing? Today the genocide mostly continues in the guise of "Defending our Common-Sense Self-Evidently True God Given Values". Or more hypocritically Zionism and the "holy Jews" (non-religious because the actual Orthodox religious Jews curse Zionism and the Israeli state as they censor Orthodox Jews who criticize in violent immoral and illegal fashion.) who almost went extinct because of Adolf Hitler. Of which Hitler, founder of the Third Reich ("Third Holy Roman Empire") allegedly got his hatred and genocide ideas from the Quran, as Christians say, and not the various contradicting Bibles that say Jews killed God/son of God, (which the Quran refutes as the Muslim Prophet Jesus never got killed) and the German Protestant Christian Theologian

Martin Luther whose words filled Nazi propaganda material without editing. Of which we must never forget the "special Holy Jews" and defend them and their military no matter what they do no matter the cost, even though we are a "Secular Rational Peace-loving Christian Nation" whose values include those taught by Muslim Prophet Jesus like giving charity to the needy, telling the truth, turning the other cheek, condemning lies, fighting against usury/interest and injustice or sinful immorality and disbelief.

Are things not clearer to see how our understanding and environment mixed with poor memories due to sin and laziness regarding research as it comes to religion can lead to such vast confusions? Then when myself, a stricter Muslim around Buffalo, NY, finds out a fake Muslim leader who was their best friend for 3 years and trained at a 4 year South African Seminary belonging to a heretical sect invented in India believes in Heresy; so, we peacefully accuse each other of being extremists. With me saying he is stupid and fake who should be fired as I offer to prove via emails/texts/ear-witness testimony and him saying about me that I'm Al-Qaeda/ISIS new Muslim idiot loner who just recently converted 6 years ago. Then other mosque leaders I explain the argument to in the Buffalo area after affliction diagnose me with magic after an exorcism and explain how that Deobandi Seminarian Sect my best friend turned rival had graduated from actually openly teaches magic in their Urdu religious books but call it *"Miracle Secret prayers revealed to holy Saints to harm your evil enemies via 'Allah' cursing them supernaturally"'* where they will have strange words and rituals to say and do to get such "Divine curses" to cause health problems. Whereas these *"Saintly Powerful Curses learned from supposed 'holy men' secretly in conversations with 'Allah' though they aren't prophets"* are specifically instructed to be done in strange places like graveyards or garbage dumps, in secret where nobody can see, with strange objects like writing certain phrases or symbols in menstrual blood or doing extremely rare to find animal sacrifices at extremely specific times in strange ways. The Muslims who can show you these filthy heretical books and the quoted pages themselves written by this heretical "Muslim" sect, though most are not available outside of the Hindi/Urdu language (though a couple are translated into English), all say these rituals are sinful polytheism by prophetic Islamic standards even if just superstition, even if no Devils are making deals with these magicians to go harm somebody's health after such "rituals" are done. Then despite having near perfect physical health for 25 years in the midst of this peaceful "argument" suddenly after 3 months of politely peacefully trying to get the rival to change his religious beliefs I accuse him publicly of being a fake Muslim heretic in the mosque during dawn prayer. I go home to write emails asking for help to get this guy fired so he loses his income and housing making him, his wife, and kids homeless incomeless instantly. About 2 hours later, while typing the exposé email I get a panic attack under suspicious circumstances. Then ever since I feel vibrations and needles in my skin occasionally that come and go over the next month as I get more paranoid and start getting crazy episodes that occur for short times without warning, that eventually lead me to accuse the rival as a magician too since I already can prove he is a 100% heretic pretending to believe in Islam for whatever reason thereby getting free housing and money he doesn't deserve to get. And does anyone from the mosque show concern that maybe a hospital visit could help? No. Not even after I tell the mosque in 2019 I had been crazy, diagnosed with a mental illness and apologized etc. I get banned from that mosque in 2017 in sinful fashion for a sinful time amount from which I'm still banned today, despite the mosque themselves firing this same heretical leader in 2024, which I said they should do in 2017 and in 2019, due to my apology email where I asked for clarity on the rival's creed if he repented or not or if I'm wrong. In 2019 due to my polite email citing my mental illness diagnosis, I got a cease-and-desist order from all communication with the mosque which Amherst police agree to arrest me if not obeyed. In 2021 an imam from another mosque talked to the rival trying to get him to have a meeting with me to resolve the issues saying it's unislamic to have banned me at all. Still the then "Muslim mosque prayer leader" refuses at all costs to meet me or allow me to return without the board of the mosque, (who issued cease and desist order) approving my return. In such a case of return then still the rival says I'm not allowed to talk to him about his heresy or say he is a heretic or cause trouble like before. And you think that type of hypocrite, is above stooping to the level of doing magic spells that could cause a rival like me to go insane? Then upon hospitalizations naively thinking religion was tolerated and discussable I admitted having crazy symptoms due to magic before nurses put their hands on me to stop me from praying. Though it seems there is now an unwritten code in Secular mental health that the word "Magic" is currently not allowed to even be written within in-patient mental health medical reports unless it is done so summarized as "delusions" and never specifically reported as "Magic" itself. Literally the patient could give an educational University level lecture to medical staff about magic for 6 hours in detail fully explaining various history, theologies and religions while citing all their sources academically and the medical report would just say, "*Tangential Delusional paranoia for 6 hours continuously. Patient is religiously preoccupied. Displays no insight into their floridly psychotic symptoms. Not able to engage in reality testing. Requires more medication and Psychoeducation.(aka more drugs and secularist psychiatric worldview brainwashing).*" And nothing else of accurate facts or relevant details would be reported for the whole 8- or 12-hour shift, and they would likely mix in a few lies about agitation or aggression too to ensure the "delusions" match the risk level as would be appropriate in psychotic folk. And if you got a beard then automatically it means poor hygiene. But surely in my case you Mental experts did the best job possible under the conditions, or so you tell insurance and yourselves for every paid bill.

Though it sounds sarcastic I am not bitter or mad at destiny, it was good for me long-term and I hope to help you benefit as much as possible as a return favor. Obviously not every claim of magic is accurate and there are cases of mental illness that are purely health issues having nothing much to do with religious causes despite the afflicted insisting upon religion as the only or main factor in their mental health or lack thereof. Yet I think due diligence was not perfectly implemented in my case. There is always room to make improvements so people do not get misdiagnosed or overmedicated and suffer more than is necessary, yet all such things that occur is destined anyways. Basically secular mental health, and to some degree at ECMC itself, is like a reckless ambulance driver who is tired while behind the wheel, rushing a patient to the hospital, speeding, in the dark, in Buffalo Blizzard conditions, while drunk from alcohol they are hiding inside as a secret because they know its unethical and unprofessional to be drunk(religiously biased/motivated) while driving at work. Then this happens again and again for every emergency psychiatric patient's trip to the hospital. What percentage of trips do you think will result in a perfect trip to the hospital where everything is done correctly as best as it could have been for the patient? How often will mistakes happen in each patient's journey that could have been prevented from the top down or the bottom up that end up harmful for the patient because the people just keep doing their job as is? If we use this analogy for every mental illness journey of every patient at the Secular ECMC Behavioral Health team from CPEP or Intake until Discharge or Death, then shouldn't a Muslim upon the divinely ordained exclusively perfectly true Salafi prophetic Islam try to help improve the process at ECMC at least a little bit? Even if the driver behind the wheel still insists on disbelieving in Islam and going to hell? Can't that driver accept some advice? Or does that driver have some type of mental illness that prevents any benefit?

I am fully aware many of you may be pissed off getting preached to by a Salafi since you are so spiritually secular, aka ill, and unaware of how spiritually ill you actually are just as a mentally ill patient in crisis cannot realize they are so wrong but the "healthy dedicated professionals with experience in this specific field" will claim they are sick and don't know it yet so must just trust the process; so it goes on as painlessly as possible to get the best possible results for everyone involved as destined. That is the role I see myself in so please don't be offended too long for too much. It's not your fault if you have been thus far, to the point of not even reading this far or calling the emergency psych police unit to bring me back immediately, because your whole life up to this point didn't prepare you well enough to actively be prepared for a spiritual crisis health improving treatment. Just as you will claim to the next Muslim or non-Muslim patient to be hospitalized whether they have magic or a regular mental health problem. So I figure since I gave you 8+ years of my time that you got paid money for preaching "mental health" to me, which is a religious activity as proven before since it involves changing or "improving" beliefs + thoughts+ emotions + behaviors all of which are religion related especially linked to good/bad or lawful/sinful since Allah will judge people for all they do their whole life and not just one hour a week on Sundays or Saturdays. For since there is no such thing as a secular post-death reality there really isn't any possible secular mental health treatment either. There can be secular medicine, this is real and useful when it is objective. Yet secularism itself is just a myth because the Christian world realized the poisonous society false religions create. So they abandoned Christianity just as Muhammad was taught by Allah to tell them to do in order to have the best result individually and collectively in this world and get paradise individually in the next. The problem was due to hundreds of years of Crusader lies the pro-Islam movement from the African slaves and foreigners was not even heard or considered when Secularism was chosen as the new religion to rule Euro-Merica which everyone is forced under penalty of law to convert to or suffer, to various degrees if they refuse. Thus the national problem-solving solution just ended up being a different problem and as you all know this "solution to Christian Sectarian rule" has caused more problems, yet Allah destined this problem perhaps to allow a bigger trickle of Islam to get into Euro-Merica than the devilish faiths of Christianity allowed. So yes, things got worse in many ways for many souls in Euro-Merica but Allah knows what the best end result is before the earth was made and before prophets were sent to warn us about the already pre-destined unavoidable end, we all will know with certain truth sooner or later willingly or unwillingly which we will meet after we die.

You can misdiagnose me and mistreat me and cause me to suffer and it is okay from my side. Maybe I misdiagnosed you all too and have misunderstood the reality of the spiritual sicknesses in the world, the mental health industry and ECMC. After reading my version of the story of my mental health illness history, do you still think you got the right diagnosis in 2017 the label/stigma of which hasn't been changed? These things are possible and not impossible to recover from if Allah destines it. Although regarding Prophet Muhammad and his mental health, nobody can afford to misdiagnose someone claiming to be the final Messenger of Allah. If/when Allah sends a final Messenger, or any prophet at all, and you get it wrong the consequences are worse than fatal results and it is the biggest mistake to ever make. Sadly as destined, it is also the hardest error to bring to people's attention so they can appropriately cure themselves from the arrogance, ignorance and laziness preventing them from gaining spiritual health, safety and prosperity for eternity. Hence no matter how offended you are at my message truly answer who has a more justified emotional injury to have? The Secular person who proudly says *"We want to help your "mental health" improve temporarily, but we don't care what happens to your soul or long-term eternity, or even your mental health once you are discharged and stop paying us money."* Or the Salafi Muslim practitioner like I claim to be imitating who says, *"I care about your religious health which affects your mental health in every way, in the short-term, mid-term and long-term and the eternal results you having poor religious/mental health will have if your sickness of ignorance, arrogance, laziness and doubt continues longer or spreads to infect others since spiritual illnesses are contagious. Even if you hate me, harm me, don't want help and make things difficult, I will still try to help you for free whenever needed as much as you allow me to as painlessly as Allah helps me do it. Or so I should say and should sincerely mean if I am destined and blessed by Allah enough to say it."* If Allah wills you now understand the truly healthy mind state that purely perfect Salafiyyah and only Salafiyyah is legitimately capable of producing in humans despite all false religions and heretical distortions of Islam doing similar talking but walking you towards a cliff that leads to a fall into eternal or temporary hellfire because of the spiritually ill leading the spiritually ill. Or the blind/dumb leading the blind/dumb not wanting to learn about Muhammad and the prophetic faith Allah sent him to teach the world from the ages of 40 until his natural peaceful death at 63 after he had miraculously united all of the Arabian Peninsula under Islam. Even though it had started out in 610 CE with him as a minority of 1 in a cave all alone just him being grabbed by Angel Gabriel and being told, "Read!" To which he said multiple times he didn't even know how to read or what to read if he did know how to read. And until Muhammad's death he never knew how to read or write his own name even, when he had to sign documents as Head of state he used a ring to seal/stamp because of his lack of writing ability. Yet Allah decreed to make the Quran more amazingly evidently Divine due to this fact of prophetic illiteracy. Truly by the Quran being brought from the tongue of an illiterate 40-year-old orphan in the Arabian Desert in the 600s CE, it is more miraculous than the truthful Muslim Virgin Mary giving birth to Muslim Prophet Jesus or his eventual return from Paradise where he went to unharmed to return later as Muhammad prophesied. This too did the Muslim Virgin Mary have a "mental illness" when she said she got pregnant without sex? And she maintained this truthful story throughout her life and insisted everyone who disbelieved her was damned to suffer eternally in Hellfire. Or did the Muslim Prophet Abraham have a "mental illness" when he became the first man to perform circumcision, starting with himself past his 80s when he was childless and promised by Allah to have kids when he was married to an old post-menopausal wife? Or did Moses the twice homeless homicidal fugitive have a "mental illness" when telling Pharaoh he is a Prophet of Allah and Pharaoh has to change his religion and politics? Or Prophet Joseph the abandoned kid found in a well, enslaved, put into prison for not fornicating, miraculously appointed to a royal position have a "mental illness" when he imposed harsh draconian austere rationing of the economy and food supply for 7 consecutive years due to an interpretation of a dream somebody else had that he says Allah taught him it means there will be a famine after 7 years that will last for 7 years? Or did prophet Noah have a "mental illness" building a warship far from the sea when he was a desperate minority religious preacher whose membership stopped increasing? Allah strengthens the truth of prophetic guidance no matter who tries to extinguish it, for the true truth is always victorious regardless of the alleged current game score even if liars lie to themselves trying to hide having knowledge of it when it is seen visibly directly in front of them. The game itself is pre-destined by Allah the Creator to fix the game so the good guys always win even if the bad guys don't know it until the game is finished. For even the good Muslim soldiers that die in battle against evil non-Muslim soldiers in a military defeat are not even technically defeated. For the dead Muslims go to paradise eventually and the dead non-Muslims to eternal hellfire after punishment in their harmful graves. So even if a few battles are lost there is no equality or fairness in this religious experience. Equality doesn't exist religiously even if secularists insist. Keeping in mind if Muhammad had a "mental illness" or worse than that in his claim to be a prophet, then how did Allah treat this alleged "false prophet and his religion"? Did his mission thrive in a manner a true prophet's would have? Or did it get crushed due to all the worldly disadvantages it had, like all falsehood always is? Is there any doubt in your diagnosis? Any need for further sincere scientific scholastically advanced studies and research on Muhammad?

The same human Muslims, known as the Sahabah (Muslims who personally met Muhammad as Muslims while he was alive) in the 600s who converted to this new Salafi Islamic faith that began with this 1 man Muhammad preaching on a daily basis to one person at a time to reach a number of 100,000+ of Muslims who personally met Muhammad in his 23 years of prophethood in the 600s CE. Of whom all his followers, those who met him and those who didn't, believed Angels sent by Allah the Creator were telling this elderly illiterate guy verses of a super intellectually advanced poetic Arabic book which thousands of them memorized, as he did, cover to cover in Arabic completely, as do millions of Muslims today. Of which many non-Muslims think and say it is music or singing when they hear the voice of a Quran reciter. These same human Sahabah who as non-Muslims say were infected with this special "mental illness" that Muhammad caught and spread like a plague virus throughout the world, decided they had to bring this "deluded crazy" medicinal message to the two countries nearest them, who at the time were the world's superpowers. The Persian Empire and the Roman/Byzantine Empire. What happened when these infected Sahabah brought Islam to these two superpowers both at the same time? I don't need to say what happened, because we will live in the present reality today taking it "day by day" when curing this spiritual sickness Allah has been healing worldwide ever since humans came to earth after they got divinely created and divided due to disagreements regarding religion.

The "popular rival spiritual medicinal opinions" many people held at that Muhammadean era until today have labeled Salafiyyah Islam as "Madness", "Bewitchment", "Demonic Possession", "Poetry", "Lies", "Forged writings copied from other religions" and sometimes all of those diagnoses combined without even attempting to hear or read or learn what that Islamic message of verses said. Many wars were fought in many ways due to the Salafi religion of Islam this man, the final Prophet Muhammad, claimed he was taught during those 23 years of Prophethood until he died as Allah destined. Further wars have been waged in many ways against the adherents and alleged adherents of this same religion, causing worldwide disunity and massive confusion since lack of sincerity and knowledge is something Allah has destined as a blessing in disguise. And many more wars will go on in many ways in the future as well due to this Salafi Islamic reformation as well, though not always seen by us as relevant or diagnosed appropriately with accuracy. Anyways as you hopefully read this Quran as I have tried to politely desperately suggest in my humblest begging method, although I said I wouldn't mention any more verses out of respect, I finally decide to end this letter for good inshallah with the following translated verses ending with a 1,420+ year still standing challenge. At the very minimum, you will better understand my "mental health crisis and allegedly unexplainably unpredictably surprisingly completely cured illness"(which I hope is not destined to return or harm me if Allah destines that is best) and be better equipped to improve the health of future Muslim patients after reading or at least increase your cultural diversity competence level, if Allah has destined such a blessing to occur. Arabic Quan's and their translations can be obtained online for free, though translation accuracy varies as true legitimate perfect Divine Revelation cannot be translated by anything except Allah and Allah did not translate any Quran because languages themselves are not designed to be translated to 100% equivalent accuracy. So, since humans cannot even be translated, anyone claiming the non-Arabic Quran is the Quran is mistaken. But similar to how you can learn medicine in English though not knowing the Latin or Greek it may have originated from, ignoring the Arabic Muslim advancements stolen by the Renaissance figures after exposure to Muslim medicine during the Crusades, knowledge of Arabic itself is not necessary to cure much of our spiritual illness as I myself to this day am not fluent in Arabic yet. May all of us get more beneficial blessings, and not be deservedly cursed, as we all continue being tested with our specially customized lessons; such as this. Before our scary promised final eternal Judgement by our 1 Creator Allah, wisely as surprisingly destined, as reported on the tongue of the final Prophet Muhammad and the earlier human prophets sent before him who have died, from who we descended with our opportunities to develop spiritually, thankfully not yet ended. I appreciate your patience for reading this long message and accepting some of this advice from a former ECMC patient. We will all meet again later as Allah has destined after we all die and decompose and get Resurrected on the Day of Terror also known as the Day of Judgement. As the English interpreted translations of the Arabic Quran say in 41:33-36,

"And who is better in speech than one who invites to Allāh and does righteousness and says, "Indeed, I am of the Muslims." The good deed and the evil deed cannot be equal. Repel (the evil) with one which is better (Allâh orders the faithful believers to be patient at the time of anger, and to excuse those who treat them badly) then verily he, between whom and you there was enmity, (will become) as though he was a close friend. But none is granted it (the above quality) except those who are patient - and none is granted it except the owner of the great portion (of happiness in the Hereafter i.e. Paradise and of a high moral character) in this world. And if there comes to you from Satan (in human or jinn form) an evil suggestion, then seek refuge in Allāh. Indeed, He(Allah) is the Hearing, the Knowing."

As the English interpreted translations of the Arabic Quran say in 4:78-83,
"Wheresoever you may be, death will overtake you even if you are in fortresses built up strong and high!" And if some good reaches them,

they say, "This is from Allâh," but if some evil befalls them, they say, "This is from you (O Muhammad)." Say: "All things are from Allâh," so what is wrong with these people that they fail to understand any word? What comes to you of good is from Allāh, but what comes to you of evil, [O man], is from yourself. And We have sent you, [O Muḥammad], to the people as a messenger, and sufficient is Allāh as Witness. He who obeys the Messenger has obeyed Allāh; but those who turn away – We have not sent you over them as a guardian. They say: "We are obedient," but when they leave you, a section of them spend all night in planning other than what you say. But Allâh records their nightly (plots). So turn aside from them (do not punish them), and put your trust in Allâh. And Allâh is Ever All-Sufficient as a Disposer of affairs. Then do they not reflect upon the Qur'ān? If it had been from [any] other than Allāh, they would have found within it much contradiction. And when there comes to them something [i.e., information] about [public] security or fear, they spread it around. But if they had referred it back to the

Messenger or to those of authority among them, then the ones who [can] draw correct conclusions from it would have known about it. And if not for the favor of Allāh upon you and His mercy, you would have followed Satan, except for a few."

As the English interpreted translations of the Arabic Quran say in 4:105-116,

"Indeed, We have revealed to you, [O Muḥammad], the Book (the Quran) in truth so you may judge between the people by that which Allāh has shown you. And do not be for the deceitful an advocate. And seek the Forgiveness of Allâh, certainly, Allâh is Ever Oft-Forgiving, Most Merciful. And do not argue on behalf of those who deceive themselves. Indeed, Allāh loves not one who is a habitually sinful deceiver. They conceal [their evil intentions and deeds] from the people, but they cannot conceal [them] from Allāh, and He is with them [in His knowledge] when they spend the night in such as He does not accept of speech. And ever is Allāh, of what they do,

encompassing. Here you are - those who argue on their behalf in [this] worldly life - but who will argue with Allāh for them on the Day of Resurrection, or who will [then] be their representative? And whoever does a wrong or wrongs himself but then seeks forgiveness of Allāh will find Allāh Forgiving and Merciful. And whoever earns [i.e., commits] a sin only earns it against himself. And Allāh is ever Knowing and Wise. But whoever earns an offense or a sin and then blames it on an innocent [person] has taken upon himself a slander and manifest sin. And if it was not for the favor of Allāh upon you, [O Muḥammad], and His mercy, a group of them would have determined to mislead you. But they do not mislead except themselves, and they will not harm you at all. And Allāh has revealed to you the Book(the Quran) and wisdom(the Sunnah as practiced/preached by the true Salafis as defined by Allah afterwards) and has taught you that which you did not know. And ever has the favor of Allāh upon you been great. No good is there in much of their private conversation, except for those who enjoin charity or that which is right or conciliation between people. And whoever does that seeking means to the approval of Allāh then We are going to give him a great reward. And whoever contradicts and opposes the Messenger (Muhammad)after the right path has been shown clearly to him, and follows other than the (true) believers' way, We shall keep him in the path he has chosen, and burn him in Hell - what an evil destination! Verily! Allâh forgives not (the sin of) setting up partners (in worship) with Him, but He forgives whom He wills sins other than that, and whoever sets up partners in worship with Allâh, has indeed strayed far away."

As the English interpreted translations of the Arabic Quran say in 2:21-27,

"O mankind, worship your Lord(Allah), who created you and those before you, that you may become righteous- [He] who made for you the earth a bed [spread out] and the sky a ceiling and sent down from the sky, rain and brought forth thereby fruits as provision for you. So do not attribute to Allāh equals while you know [that there is nothing similar to Him]. And if you (Arab pagans, Jews, and Christians, any/all of the non-Muslims) are in doubt concerning that which We have sent down (i.e. the Qur'an + Sunnah) to Our slave (Muhammad), then produce a Surah(chapter) of the like thereof (Meaning bring 1 chapter on any nearby level comparable to the Arabic Quran! The smallest chapter is 10 words long) and call (all) your witnesses (supporters and helpers) besides Allâh, if you are truthful (meaning get help to meet this literary challenge from any Humans +Jinnis + Angels + Creatures + Ghosts or alleged deities of all time all combined). But if you do it not, and you can never do it, then fear the Fire (Hell) whose fuel is men and stones, prepared for the disbelievers. And give good tidings to those who believe and do righteous deeds that they will have gardens [in Paradise] beneath which rivers flow. Whenever they are provided with a provision of fruit therefrom, they will say, "This is what we were provided with before." And it is given to them in likeness. And they will have therein purified spouses, and they will abide therein eternally. Indeed, Allāh is not timid to present an example - that of a mosquito or what is smaller than it. And those who have (truly) believed know that it is the truth from their Lord. But as for those who disbelieve, they say, "What did Allāh intend by this as an example?" He(Allah) misleads many thereby and guides many thereby. And He(Allah) misleads not except the defiantly disobedient, who break the covenant of Allāh after contracting it and sever that which Allāh has ordered to be joined and cause corruption on earth. It is those who are the losers."

And thus was the end of this letter destined to become this book finished, as of Friday January 16th, 2026 around noon prior to me going to the Jumuah prayer. Did I seem crazy or psychotic to you? Most of this book thus far, aside from some pre-publication editing like spelling corrections, was typed between Dawn and noon on that same day. Should I be hospitalized based on what I wrote? Should my medicine be increased from zero to a high dose of 25 milligrams per day? No? What about 12 hours later? That very night Allah had destined that despite my plans of having my final ECMC appointment ever on February 4th, 2026 soundly proving my health without medicine. I would be surprisingly hospitalized "voluntarily" when the police who were twice called to my non-Muslim parents' house offered me no options other than going "voluntarily" or involuntarily to the ECMC hospital for "psychiatric evaluations" in CPEP. Some of you may already know something about the oppressive illegal situation that medical staff escalated upon me during such a "voluntary" visit that resulted in me getting sentenced by a hospital judge to involuntarily take anti-psychotic medicine 13 days later. This occurred despite me being illegally held with medical record forgery committed and refusing all brain medications for nearly 2 weeks while remaining as sane and peaceful as was destined throughout. Nevertheless, after this unexpected uncomfortable ECMC experience from January 17th until February 9th 2026 for a total of 24 days, I was discharged and told by the perjurious doctor days earlier that I'd have to accept my labeled illness from 2017 and take a shot monthly for the rest of my life due to the highly paid Hospital Judge's orders. Many healthcare professionals concurred and were ready to continue my shot treatment. But my eventual escape from such a fate and return to non-medicated healthy life is not the subject of this book.

That exciting journey of going off medicine on November 11th, 2025 to going back to the hospital to explain why/how I was performing an emergency Islamic Exorcism in self-defense on my mother on the night of January 16th, 2026, the same technical day after which I wrote most of this book in nearly one sitting, will be told in another book inshallah when the many still pending 12 legal cases at the Justice Center alleging illegal abuse and perjury are concluded inshallah. And hopefully the magicians I met inside the hospital, who actually confessed to doing magic as they were caught on camera during our spiritual battling, prior to us all getting discharged, as secular medicine diagnoses confessed magicians caught on camera as "delusional", repent and embrace Islam inshallah. Although sadly those 12 legal cases pending resolution against your colleagues may delay the delivery of this book to you, lest I ruin my battle against malpractice criminals by inviting their coworkers too soon and truthfully talking about my experience(s) with magic even slightly, as alluded to before. My apologies for the delay of conveying the soul-saving message. Yet now I know and can prove that despite the unprofessional and discriminatory diagnosis in 2017 and unethical unprofessional illegal manner in which I was forced to take medicine again in 2026, which cannot be safely stopped for months if not years, I do not have the mental illness I was labeled with and am perhaps healthy mentally. At least I know now I don't need medicine of the type you prescribe. Perhaps in 2017 I had a 'brief psychotic disorder' sometimes which can last for less than 1 day or less than 1 month at a time then doesn't ordinarily reoccur. Or perhaps I have Schizotypal personality which can result in Psychosis when extremely stressed which goes away without any medicine ever needed. Or even if I had an illness after 5 years without an episode the brain can heal completely from neuroplasticity aka Allah's blessed self-repairing design of the brain. But if you ask me, it was magic that triggered medication treatment both times that I have now recovered from as will be proven later. Yet since 2024, the medical industry has invented blood tests which are available to determine the amount of psychosis someone actively has. In effect rendering much of the current psychiatric guesswork obsolete from what I understand. So rather than a 15-minute conversation with a disbeliever making the decision regarding whether I am crazy or not or mentally diseased in need of medication, now we can just test the blood and examine the biomarkers in RNA over time to see how crazy I am and how it changes. When combined with gene testing of DNA we can even determine which medicine is best for my genetic profile and which dosage of medicine is best as well as the craziness levels which fluctuate over time. Rather than the crude archaic cave-man type of psychiatric slogan, *"Crazy one time in life? Take Pills Forever!!"* Additionally, I would've included my own test results in this book as proof but figure that's HIPAA data and I don't desire my enemies knowing my health data either, though we only fear harm from Allah.

Also since that 2026 hospitalization experience and how certain doctors like Dr. G and others interacted then I have removed some from my list of intended recipients, despite keeping some of their history in the book. This is because it seems they are insincere and uninterested in this matter of faith and proved themselves unethical in the past despite my efforts at dialog. At least I feel I am not the right messenger to such people if any messenger at all can ever trigger their guidance if Allah destines such a blessing.

Anyways despite the past oppression as destined by Allah to have occurred in ECMC inpatient zones, and partially because the options for Muslim Shariah compliant mental healthcare are limited, I have decided to continue treating at ECMC for a while or until Allah provides escape to the lands of the Muslims where I can obtain proper healthcare. Why? Definitely not because of your services. If it were up to me ECMC would never see me again or get any payment at all. Yet it is only because of the rights of my non-Muslim parents and obedience to them being such an obligatory duty that I continue to treat with the outpatient staff there. Despite other inpatient staff members committing provable perjury when legally under oath to tell the truth in Hospital Court and some doctors/nurses proven to have forged medical records to put me on such a high medicine dose involuntarily unethically and illegally doing so in ECMC's name, with others guilty of abuse and neglect, not all of you are guilty in these crimes. Whereas since my parents are dutifully due my obedience and it doesn't seem you can or will harm me too much then rather than obtain telehealth care from some non-ECMC services, as I desired, I will give you a chance to prove you are innocent of the crimes of your colleagues and take a chance of having a mutually beneficial mental health relationship. Why? Because good treatment to parents is that important and the mental health standards of Shariah law, which Muslims are supposed to follow even in Kafir countries, are greater than the highest secular ideals or even the greatest non-Muslim ideals. Simply put, the Islamic Muslims have more moral standards.

As a disclaimer do not take my book/case as medical advice or research for making your own decisions in your own particular cases magical or medical. My case/health is different than everyone else. There is no one size fits all when it comes to mental, physical or spiritual health aside from general guidance like Islamic Salafiyyah being the cure for spiritual health issues. Salafiyyah was explained in more depth in the previously written memoir so we will not reexplain it here. Although for those unfamiliar with it we will say a few things to clarify, in case you are unaware. Salafi Islam is the pure prophetic religion of Islam without any type of blind following of non-prophetic personalities. Salafiyyah is based on the understanding of the Sahabah (companions of Muhammad) and the Salaf (Pious Muslim predecessors who lived and died according to the blessed religion of Islam as taught by Muhammad and his original Companions/Sahabah). Anyone alive can err and go astray so following anyone today must be through textual evidences that have a foundation in prophetic revelation primarily. There are nuances within the religion's jurisprudence yet overall most of Islam is fundamentally finalized in something more concrete than stone, Allah's perfect unchangeable decree itself of having perfected the religion of Islam which he chose for us all to practice. Hence no Bida or additions/subtractions/distortion/inventions are allowed regarding the religious matters. The problem is all heretics who claim to be Muslims, and there are many, as well as many ordinary non-heretical Muslims often fall into such inventive Bida. This often causes community disunity, as it should. When it is a matter between truth and falsehood in terms of religious beliefs and practices people and jinn must pick a side. Sadly, many get confused and choose wrongly then combat the side of correctness until they are defeated or get a temporary illusionary victory against the blessed sect of Salafis whom Allah himself protects and gives true victory to despite the plots of all the wicked ones who plot. The main test though is the timing of such victory and the recognition of it often is veiled so much so that many times even the striving Salafi themselves cannot see how they are victorious against the oppression or oppressive foes. And sometimes it's better for you and everyone else to believe you have lost the battle/war before you die, or even afterwards, than to see your triumphant victory is true.

Again, as a disclaimer I must make it clear that not every mental illness is caused by magic. And not every claim of magic is truthful or provable and sometimes mental illnesses can mimic magic and mental auto-suggestion can make someone believe an affliction is magic when it is in fact a purely biological mental illness destined by Allah to occur. Every case is truly extremely unique so please don't practice medicine or make medical decisions based exclusively on what you read in this non-fiction book by me. However, with that said even though not every insanity is magic even if the insane person says it is, there are a certain % of cases that are magic or possession. So then what is ECMC's ratio of

crazy to magic diagnoses? Meaning what % of
cases get labeled as magic by ECMC staff, or any
staff at any Secular healthcare institution? And
how often does it get cured? Also how many
times does insurance get billed for a case of
magic? If these numbers are zero then that is a
complete distortion and aberration from reality.
Clinical evidence proves that number can never
be zero historically over a long period of time.
Unless secular interests or financial billing
reasons dictate that number must be zero
though reality indicates a higher number is
correct. Magic is well-known in every religion.
Simply put if any God exists then so does magic.
Also magic is known from history as real. So
when did magic ever go extinct anywhere?
Americans are taught about the Salem witch
trials in the 1600s where ignorant colonist
extremist Christians went overboard and killed
innocents in their hunt to exterminate magicians.
But just because a few idiots abused the "Justice
System" of Colonial America, does that mean
magic never existed or ceased to function
globally? No. And even if America eradicated
magic in the 1600s, though some Christian

denominations themselves practice forms of magic, surely later immigrants legal and otherwise may have included some magicians amongst them. Or do they screen people for being magicians at the border and censor all possibilities of learning magic in Secular lands? Do Secular countries even have a system setup to deal with magic at all? Not really. So because of incompetence and actual conspiracy in some areas of society the only solution Secularism has for magic is denial. They couldn't even ban alcohol in America during the prohibition era! So do you think the USA can organize a campaign against magicians when freedom reigns in totality allowing magic to spread as a religious freedom and a useful tool for those who know it is real? There is no big magic conspiracy that I know of, for magicians are more comparable to street gangs and independent thugs than organized united government departments. Just because magicians, like most criminals, often conspire in secrecy, to then claim magic itself doesn't exist because it is usually done secretly is the same as claiming crime went extinct and is impossible to occur. Magical rituals while pure placebo superstition from a theological aspect, can sometimes harm humans or jinn if Allah allows such rituals to result in their intended damage. Those who know this fact know and those who don't are either in denial or distracted. The point is magic is present in some cases that get psychiatric treatment. It doesn't have to be mine or many that you encounter, but some are indeed misdiagnosed and overmedicated. Even without magic in the picture many people get overmedicated and misdiagnosed. And due to the harm such mistakes cause, nobody can ever afford such mistakes to occur. Yet as it is now it is very easy the way Psychiatry is currently functioning for abusive overmedication and misdiagnosis to occur for religious, racist, sexist, patriotic, financial, and all other evil kinds of reasons systematically. Those in the lab coats with hospital badges and degrees are often blinded by the credentials to think any and every patient is there because they are ill and they cannot be trusted due to their illness as has been observed and diagnosed most likely before you ever met them. Basically if you are healthy in a psychiatric setting without a badge then you are guilty without trial just because you are there. Especially if you claim to be an Exorcist or use the phrase "magic". Saying the word "magic" is practically coded as "give medicine" in most psychiatric minds. Whereas a bad psychiatric file with a mistake is even more harmful than a bad police record with a mistake, because bad psychiatric notes can but you in pill prison for life while police jail is usually temporary. This paragraph is meant to help you realize magic never went extinct and the mental industry is not immune from magic even if the Secular statistics suggest it is due to historically incomplete medical understandings. Magic is a verifiable reality researchable and most importantly curable through prophetic methods. Thus I don't care so much if you disbelieve my claim that magic likely caused my initial insanity that got mislabeled twice, first in 2017 and again via illegal perjury and forged medical notes in 2026, because it's much better to be overmedicated without magic than to be "healthy" without medicine while afflicted with magic unknowingly. Magic is worse than most diseases especially if untreated via ignorance, insincerity or denial.

But it's not about me, is it? No, it never was and never should be. It's not even about magic either. It is really about the Prophet Muhammad and his message of Islamic Salafiyyah. Was he mentally ill too? Yes or no and why? Was he truthful or a liar? Yes or no and why? If Muhammad is not mentally ill, nor a liar, then what is the diagnosis of the alleged final prophet of God? Isn't it professionally irresponsible for someone to practice mental health improvement without knowing about him? Especially considering that mental health or behavioral health, whatever you want to call it, is the most religious type of healthcare there is. For prophets and religions of all types only came to change mental health for the better and change behaviors for the better for all of time. So truly am I the mentally ill person in need of medicine? Maybe. But isn't everyone in need of a spiritual medicine to improve mentalities, emotions and actions? What dose and delivery method is correct for me? And what dose of spiritual medicine is correct for you?

During every Friday Khutbah (Sermon) everyone present hears the same message with the same exact words. Yet somehow every person hearing that identical sermon in an identical setting will get different levels of benefits/blessings from what all of them equally heard of religious speech. Memory is not the factor causing this difference of effect from a multi-party experienced identical cause. Many people will quote the same exact words which all heard yet differ in their understanding of the message, sometimes gaining benefits the speaker didn't even intend or consider possible from the words conveyed. Others may fall into disastrous distortions of doctrine due to their own diseases. Of which mental health plays a great role in your personal religion from a religious understanding doesn't it? Likewise religion will and does play a great role in your mental health from an objective mental health perspective, doesn't it? By which I mean to say the medicine dosage and its effects greatly impact me differently based on my faith. For the more sins I do the lower my faith is, and the more good deeds I do the higher it rises. But what does that have to do with brain pills? So much that you can never understand. For when I was initially on 15 mg, I blamed that pill for everything negative about my post-diagnosis lifestyle when in reality I just lacked discipline to be Islamic after hospitalization in 2017 being forced to live with non-Muslim parents far from all local masjids. It's a lot easier to be Islamic when in hermit-like isolation near or in a masjid but much harder to do so when daily interactions with kafir kin are unavoidable and sinful options of entertainment are available with ease. So when I blamed a pill for fatigue to justify sins like TV then I digressed religiously making me feel worse about everything. Which I used as fuel to decline further, "all because of the 15 mg pill". When I was blessed to take tiny steps back to fully practicing my faith as before, 4 years after my initial diagnosis by eliminating TV totally from my life, once again as it did the first time I quit TV, in 2021 my life drastically improved despite no medicine change until later that year. For Allah doesn't change an external condition until we change our own inner condition. Eventually I titrated down to zero over the years and then got back in the hospital as previously mentioned. But today as I write I still have both a shot in my system approximately releasing 15 mg a day and a daily pill of 10 mg. Meaning I am basically on 25 mg of a medicine that devasted me in 2018 on 15 mg and later when on 10 mg as well. But it was never the medicine that harmed me, it was my sins as Allah defines them in Islamic Shariah for me personally that caused all the symptoms of my health. For technically it is not possible in 2026 today to be on 5 times as much of a sedative medicine than I was on from 2023 to 2025, on a non-therapeutic dosage then I might add, and feel better in all regards concerning mentality and energy and everything that makes a person a human. For years I blamed the medicine for energy or memory or mood instead of blaming my own religion level. Yet the molecules of the medicine do not have power to change anything unless the Creator of my body allows such changes to occur. Consider yourself and how many patients react differently to different medicines and dosages yet all are human with "mental illnesses". Sometimes there are even different medicinal reactions with the same patient. One day they may react well with medicine and the next they will not, or any other various variable reactions can occur.

Millions can have the same exact mental illness diagnosis and be professionally well-treated with the same exact medicine and dosage, but their personal lives and the influence that pill will have on them differs so much it is as if all of them had different customized medicines only taken by them, despite so much matching factors. Why? This is because of their different religious levels concerning their good deeds and bad deeds. It almost sounds crazy to postulate until you actually live it yourself and go through dark sinful days on low medicine then manage to rise above it to acquire health and then get a high dosage that you almost don't even notice because you aren't doing those same sins anymore in life. Sins are a symptom of a spiritual illness and the spiritual illnesses have co-occurring disorders including mental illnesses and lethargy or depression and many types of evils too many for any human to ever possibly list, for Allah punishes sins as destined for those unblessed and not showered with Allah's mercy to be safe and/or forgiven without many consequences. As an additional example of the spiritual reality being more impactful than medication and potentially nullifying the effects of medication, take a look at this book and its impact on readers. Will every reader react the same? Why not? Do they not all receive an identical message? Are they not all intelligent free-willed creatures? Why then will some believe and others disbelieve in Islamic Salafiyyah with those who do believe differing in their practice of it? Well for one the faith of equality is mythological. But the reality aside from that fact, is that medicine whether chemical or spiritual or any other substance in any type of form can only do what the Creator of everything destined to occur. Nothing will overcome the power of Allah or the plans of Allah to make the truth of Salafiyyah, and by that I mean the true Salafiyyah not just anyone calling to the name via labels that are not accurate, totally dominant and victorious over all other faiths even if those faiths hide their religion and pretend to be secular in design or practice. Meaning "Secular Mental Health" will eventually bow to Islam sooner or later because falsehood and half-truths never last long without ultimately decomposing and dying out even if it happens slowly. Yet the destined end of Secularism and its prideful mental health experiments may not occur in our own lifetimes. So why fight for a cause that will not benefit you in your graveyard? Whereas a mistake in spiritual health by ignoring the reality of a soul and religious realities when treating "mental health" is practicing religious therapy in disguise cloaking it with lies of every size even if you didn't or still won't recognize it.

For example, upon my perusal of recent medical records my hospitalization for alleged psychosis in 2026 of 24 days doesn't even mention the word magic once, if I correctly read and remember, despite me mentioning it often daily. Hence my theory that it became part of Secular medical practice that the "M-word" cannot even be written down in medical reports anymore as if it is a taboo codified as "delusions" or "paranoia" instead. Or my most favorite medical codewords: "religiously preoccupied". Meaning someone is too religious for your hypersensitive secular defective tastebuds. Such a term and coding system is not and never can be religiously neutral as long as emotional humans are dictating the notes. It really is a simple as this, non-Muslims historically abuse Muslims for religious reasons, but they can't legally do that as easily anymore everywhere, yet they can do so in certain settings like prison or more creative circumstances like psychiatric settings. So a Muslim saying the "M-word" has no truly fair opportunity for genuine respectful evaluation from Secular non-Muslims in a crisis-centric setting. It's comparable to a Single Virgin Homosexual therapist treating a Heterosexual married couple for family counseling under the premise that as a "professional" counselor their homosexuality has no negative impact regarding them "improving" the mental health of the heterosexual couple and their marriage/family. So basically any situation whatever that leads a Muslim to be "checked for craziness" by disbelievers pretty much has a foregone conclusion they will be labeled as such due to unadmitted bias from the staff concerning what is a healthy level of religiosity. And that is where "religious preoccupation" and similar terms combined with deliberately snippeted out of context quotes can create a very ugly case history indeed. Where anyone can be crazy on paper from a mental health perspective if you got enough religious haters writing about your healthcare. Especially Lazy nurses with experience who customarily write minimal notes just looking for crazy context, so as to comply with what is expected of them to write down *"documenting delusions and religious preoccupation".* Yet even if we dismiss the facts of compounded prejudice due to religious opinions of humans being unavoidable, currently many patients are treated as meat-based moneybags that are to be drained via dosing and diagnosing them in the most lucrative way possible. It's not really in the hospitals interest to discharge a "impatient crazy patient" when it is too easy to keep the bill skyrocketing, most of the time such patients only get discharged to make room for new patients anyways not because of actual improvement that couldn't have been detected earlier. It's just because of overflowing "craziness" in secular society requiring patients to be discharged quickly due to need for extra bedrooms that you can't keep people for observation as much as they "truly need". For secular medicine is a business in every aspect, though mental health in particular is a religious sector of that business. Instead of being secular medical professionals you should be sincere human people. Otherwise, if you insist on treating any/all patients as a secular medical professional instead of as a morally biased religious human, then you are not even worth the ink in a period. This is because such a version of humanity is insanely inhumane. Not even animals practice secularism let alone preach it as a possibility. Secular mental health is impossible! The deniers of this reality would likely not even read this far due to arrogant anti-religiosity. This denial would even occur despite fully knowing the Hippocratic Oath, or Lasagna Oath, or even the Declaration of Geneva more common among secular medicine nowadays and binding themselves to such ritualistic ceremonial religious notions to get licensed to practice "mental health medicine" as part of the psychiatrick disassembly and reassembly lines. Such extremist secular dogmas that prevent education betray the religious oaths such professionals have taken in the name of helping human health. Whereas truthfully "the

difference between healthcare and true care" in
mental health is the difference between secular
treatment and religious treatment. Will you not
reflect and repent? For those who do perhaps
you have merit within your soul still that Allah
may bless even more than you expect.

I'm not saying you have to automatically quit but
secularist life is a hollow theory that contradicts
human reality. Nothing in life is secular
according not to just me but according to the
Divine Judge and Creator of everything. There is
not 1 minute of time that our Lord will say "that
was secular activity, so it's neither a good or bad
deed since 'free time' isn't judged by God". There
is no "free time" or "Secular time", all time is a
blessed gift and test for all of time. So don't
expect a prize for "improving mental health"
without considering it a religious activity. I'm not
saying only Muslims can benefit others because
such a theory would go against reality as well.
Yet most mental health improvements in
humans are going to always be from making
religion improvements and not physiological
chemical changes. Meaning in plain summary

that no pill will ever solve a sinner's problems. And no pill will ever harm anyone Allah protects. The problem is we give credit to the wrong things. Especially when it comes to discussing mental health or health in general in any discussions on that subject. Every doctor and person in general attributes health to everything except a sinful lifestyle. I'm not saying being sinless makes somebody immortal, and I'm not sinless either, but how many people ever tried it before to see if actually coming close to being sinless made their physical body health improve amazingly? It's a simple formula we all claim to follow but those who actually comply with prophetic medicine for our soul are few because hypocrites are the majority amongst both Muslims and disbelievers. So if people actually tried truthfully following their beliefs, they would witness things science and medicine cannot explain. The disbelievers would suffer or change since practicing disbelief ends in doom. While the Muslims if they actually did what they say they do with full conviction and truth would not be in the situations they are in today. In fact, I might not even be writing this book if the majority or even half of us "Muslims" actually walked upon the straight path we constantly ask to be guided to when talking to our Creator in our obligatory 5 daily Salat.

At the end of this initial discussion on the subject of mental health and mental illness it must be admitted and recognized even under secular guises that the field of mentality improvement is a very religiously relevant sector indeed. For religion and mental health/illnesses are synonymous no matter how many secularists say otherwise. <u>Mental Health improvement is a primary defined goal of all the world's religions</u>. So, when I do come to you for "mental health behavioral services" at least have the honesty to admit we are there to talk about religion and become a better soul. Because otherwise under the guise of Secular unbiased non-religiosity it will not help me much and it will make it much harder for me to help you as well. Therefore if you don't want to admit you are in a deeply religious healthcare sector doing extremely religious character reformation work, then I advise you to either stop lying to yourself or change industries and careers. Finally, I invite you to research Islam properly and if you were sincere and equipped with knowledge you would naturally embrace Islam becoming Salafi yourselves as would be a blessed thing for as long as such a rare blessing lasts for. Because otherwise even if you were claimants to Islam or claimed to be Muslim, if you aren't Salafi in reality then your soul is sick, your mind is malfunctioning and you will be spiritually ill. Though even real Salafis don't always match the label, we at least have the blessed formula for good health and an opportunity to heal our soul by fixing our life before we die with our destiny unknown; although Allah's promises are true. Yet still I know many are not destined to have such a blessing though we invite them politely regardless. The reason I invite you is supposed to be because I want to be free from blame when you do meet your final fate whatever that may be, and to please the Creator who made us all and demanded we repeat prophet Muhammad's call.

As the English interpreted translations of the Arabic Quran say in 41:52,

Say: "Tell me, if it (the Arabic Quran) is from Allah, and you disbelieve in it? Who is more astray than one who is in opposition far away (from the truth).

As the English interpreted translations of the Arabic Quran say in 6:111,

"And even if We had sent down to them the angels [with the message] and the dead spoke to them [of it] and We gathered together every [created] thing in front of them, they would not believe unless Allah should will. But most of them behave ignorantly."

As the English interpreted translations of the Arabic Quran say in 34:46-54,

Say, "I only advise you to do only one [thing] - that you stand for Allāh, [seeking truth] in pairs and individually, and then give thought." There is not in your companion (Prophet Muhammad) any madness. He is only a warner to you before a severe punishment.

Say, "Whatever payment I might have asked of you - it is yours. My payment is only from Allāh, and He is, over all things, Witness." Say, "Surely my Lord hurls the truth against falsehood. He is the Knower of all unseen." Say, "The truth has come, and falsehood can neither create anything nor resurrect anything. Say: "If (even) I go astray, I shall stray only to my own loss. But if I remain guided, it is because of the Revelation of my Lord to me. Truly, He is All-Hearer, Ever Near (to all things)." And if you could see when they are terrified but there is no escape, and they will be seized from a place nearby. And they will say (in the Hereafter): "We do believe (now):" but how could they receive (Faith and the acceptance of their repentance by Allâh) from a place so far off (i.e. to return to the worldly life again). Indeed they did disbelieve (in the Oneness of Allâh, Islâm, the Qur'an and Muhammad) before (in this world), and they (used to) conjecture about the Unseen [i.e. the Hereafter, Hell, Paradise, Resurrection and the Promise of Allâh (by saying) all that is untrue], from a far place. And a barrier will be set between them and that which they desire [i.e. At-Taubah (turning to Allâh in repentance) and the accepting of Faith], as was done in the past with the people of their kind. Verily, they have been in grave doubt(denial).

As the English interpreted translations of the Arabic Quran say in 20:135,

"Say, "Each [of us] is waiting; so wait. For you will know who are the companions of the sound (true) path and who is guided."

I have invited you despite my risk and potential harm to your arrogance backfiring, to personally sincerely research; as if your soul depended on it. Then you can make a better choice about belief or disbelief. Whereas from an objective professional point of view, if that's all you care about, such scrupulous study of Islam will make you better equipped to understand the world's Muslim population of billions and additionally the non-Muslim population too, as the Quran is the final message from the one who created us all. So the call to prophetic Islamic Salafiyyah has been initiated, will you heroically rise to eternal heaven or fall far down to disgrace in eternal hellfire? You have been both simultaneously begged to get Allah's mercy via a rope to Islamic salvation and warned from Allah's punishment. May Allah, our one and only Creator, bless those seeking true mental health improvement and protect them from all illness.

www.ingramcontent.com/pod-product-compliance
Lightning Source LLC
Chambersburg PA
CBHW072332150726
47998CB00017B/507